PRAISE FOR
WIFE | DAUGHTER | SELF

"Kephart's *Wife | Daughter | Self* passes the whole of a life through the prism of intimate relations and the result is revelatory: a memoir that assembles itself as we read, until all its parts are shimmering with meaning and that most sought, most elusive treasure is revealed: what it means to be human, and aware."
—Carolyn Forché, author of *What You Have Heard Is True*

"Opening Beth Kephart's memoir feels akin to stepping into a river of striking clarity and song. With tenacious honesty, *Wife | Daughter | Self* explores the weight and shape of the ever-deepening bonds we form with those closest to us and how those bonds intertwine with our perceptions of our innermost selves. This book is a journey into a life dedicated to writing and art, one that honors both joy and pain, love and loss. Piercing, lyrical, and wondrously alive with detail, Kephart's sentences sing. I didn't want it to end."
—Chloe Honum, author of *Then Winter*

158
186

"Rare and brave and beautifully written, *Wife | Daughter | Self* is a memoir to savor. Beth Kephart is a jeweler: her words glisten, the emotions shine. This story of marriage, daughterhood, and motherhood is also the story of an artist—how a woman becomes a writer and how she enters into conversation with the world. This moving work will linger with readers long after the final page."
—Diana Abu-Jaber, author of *The Language of Baklava*

"Relentless exploration of self, with sentences that will stop your heart with their exactness."
—Leslie Pietrzyk, author of *Silver Girl*

"Beth Kephart has written a riveting, atmospheric dream of a book. It's a big, complicated portrait of a woman inhabiting the major roles of her life. Sometimes we encounter Beth's 'tip-toe self,' artfully and gracefully telling her story. Other times she's out there—bold, making noise, 'piercing the truth.' But she never settles for the easy answer. She's really just asking bone-deep, tough questions. Questions that turn everything back to her readers so that we can learn how to inhabit our own roles. This memoir is so revelatory, so affecting, that long after you turn the last page, you won't stop thinking about it."

—Judy Goldman, author of *Together: A Memoir of a Marriage and a Medical Mishap*

ADDITIONAL PRAISE

"Beth Kephart . . . is a gifted, even poetic writer."

—*The New York Times Book Review*

"Kephart's writing is so clear, so nonpreachy, that you just want to jump in and join her."

—*Los Angeles Times Book Review*

"Richly evocative prose that can only be called masterful . . . a revelation and a feast."

—Andre Dubus III, author of *House of Sand and Fog*

"Writing as brilliantly as she does about love might have been enough even for someone of her intelligence and depth. But in this memoir she demonstrates that she can go further. Kephart is able to generalize from her personal experience to the greater human one."

—Wendy Gimble, *Washington Post*

"A gorgeous meditation on memoir."

—*Library Journal*

wife|daughter|self

beth kephart

FOREST AVENUE PRESS
Portland, Oregon

Name: Kephart, Beth, author.
Title: Wife, daughter, self / Beth Kephart; William Sulit, illustrator.
    Description: Portland, Oregon: Forest Avenue Press, [2021] | Summary: "Curiously, inventively, Beth Kephart reflects on the iterative, composite self in her new memoir--traveling to lakes and rivers, New Mexico and Mexico, the icy waters of Alaska and a hot-air balloon launch in search of understanding. She is accompanied, often, by her Salvadoran-artist husband. She spends time, a lot of time, with her widowed father. As she looks at them she ponders herself and comes to terms with the person she is still becoming. At once sweeping and intimate, Wife | Daughter | Self is a memoir built of interlocking essays by an acclaimed author, teacher, and critic."-- Provided by publisher.
Identifiers: LCCN 2020041314 (print) | LCCN 2020041315 (ebook)
    | ISBN 9781942436447 (paperback) | ISBN 9781942436454 (epub)
Subjects: LCSH: Kephart, Beth. | Authors, American--21st century--Biography. | LCGFT: Essays.
Classification: LCC PS3611.E695 Z46 2021 (print) | LCC PS3611.
    E695 (ebook) | DDC 813/.6 [B]--dc23
LC record available at https://lccn.loc.gov/2020041314
LC ebook record available at https://lccn.loc.gov/2020041315

Distributed by Publishers Group West

Printed in the United States

1 2 3 4 5 6 7 8 9

Forest Avenue Press LLC
P.O. Box 80134
Portland, OR 97280
forestavenuepress.com

For Bill. Of course.

In memory of my father.

CONTENTS

| WIFE |

| DAUGHTER |

| SELF |

| AFTER | WORD | 235

WIFE |
DAUGHTER |
SELF

| *wife* |

First a room. Then two rooms. Then a three-room, three-floor house. Then two stories with a porch plopped along the railroad tracks, big enough to hold a child (just one child). Then another house that got fat with things until we counted what we needed and didn't need much of that. You are an artist. I am a writer. We'll make something. Why not?

I'll leave you alone when you want alone. I'll be near when near is better. At the breakfast table, where the folded laundry spills. On the floor, in the purple light of the TV. In the bed, sometimes. Beneath the scorch of stars. By the canal, where what I want for you is the blue heron, the slick turtle, the skin that the snake left, and where you say: How much farther will we walk, how many miles are we going? I order inexpensively, so do you. I cower for traditions, you neglect them. I burn my hand on the cast-iron pan of the Valentine's Day risotto, and you fill the bowl with ice all through the night while the pain strikes the nerves like lightning theater.

We are not Virginia and Leonard. We are not Zelda and F. Scott. We are not Georgia and Alfred, Frida and Diego, Lee and Jackson, Joan and John. Still, we are original because we are original, and because I cry at every wedding, imagining again the start of things, imagining the end, the grief preordained for one or the other of us, not that there haven't already been endings, not that we haven't already recovered. We knew to recover. We recovered for the sake of us.

(We told ourselves that we recovered for our son, but I'm increasingly inclined toward honesty: We recovered for ourselves.)

"Love is not the whole of a man's life . . ." C. S. Lewis tried to convince himself. "Then comes a sudden jab of red-hot memory and all this 'commonsense' vanishes like an ant in the mouth of a furnace."

I write as wife. I write as your wife in this room of your things—your four clay teapots pointing their snouts southeast, the guitar I bought that you won't play for me, your flimsy jacket with its crumply rolled sleeves on the back of the chair that slides. The shavings of your pencils dust the carpet. The old slab of wood we bought to replace the rotted mantel lies on the floor where you have left it beside the picture you have drawn showing how to hang it with the metal brackets you are proud of—linseed-oil rubbed. I write because yesterday I found you kneeling in this midst, and you looked so young, you looked so happy, with the possibility of wood, brackets, sketches, and because once you drove me across the country so that I might have a story that I wanted, and because I remember how I almost didn't marry you, and how you almost did not stay.

Wife is a negotiation of a word. (Changing my name, unchanging my name.) Wife is a collaboration. (Let's make the words first. No? Then go ahead, make the pictures.) Wife is defenseless and defended, the silence of détente and the silence of agreement, the private acts and jealousies, never the end, sometimes beginnings. Wife, meaning yours, which now I will be, don't you leave me, don't you dare, there are ants, there is a furnace.

LILY LAKE

It's not hard to be good at kayaking across a smooth-topped lake on a puff-sky day, but I am actually so good. The yellow blades of my paddles are dragonfly wings. My biceps prettily swell. In the woods beyond there are bears and snakes, but in the split pea-pod shell of a borrowed kayak, the lake fish will not bite you.

I stop the kayak at the slanted wooden dock. I am that good at docking. I can't lift the shell to its hold without my husband's help, and so he helps me. Seventy-five feet up, past the pale-pink pop of rhododendron trees, over the heads of swishy ferns, farther than the flat rocks where (we'll learn) a copperhead once struck, stands the cottage of the lake. Beyond that is the house to which the cottage belongs, and here's what I know about that house: It was an ice house before it became a summer house, before the men and women of coal, kielbasa, and window shades transformed it with their muscle and imagination.

What should we do for our anniversary? my husband had said. He'd clicked his way to HomeAway. He'd clicked through pictures. *That one*, we'd said, of the cottage of Lily Lake. That's how we decided.

Our first night here it stormed a mighty storm. From our tree-top perch in a screened-in porch we watched the big trees bend and the pale pinks pop and the lake bruise up and dimple. Small particles of rain broke through the screen and refreshed our skin and sometimes we watched and sometimes we read and sometimes my husband fixed the Ugly Stiks for the next day's fishing. Bob. Hook. Weight. Reel. The rest of the cottage stayed dry. The pristine walls and elastic windowshades. The newly varnished floor and the turtle shell someone had left as decoration. The lids to the pots in the drawer in the kitchen. The sketch inside a frame. We left the porch, eventually, for the room upstairs, an A-ceilinged affair, planked like a floor. We lay in separate beds, which were all-white beds, listening to the running of the rain. It was an all-night performance. The room smelled of split wood. By morning the rain was gone, and the kayak powered forth, and after that my husband taught me to fish with the smallest Ugly Stik, and we stood on the dock casting our lines across the lilies of the lake.

Most of the lilies bloomed white. One, near us, bloomed yellow.

Encyclopaedia Britannica: "Most species of water lilies have rounded, variously notched, waxy-coated leaves on long stalks that contain many air spaces and float in quiet freshwater habitats. The stalks arise from thick, fleshy, creeping underwater stems that are buried in the mud. The showy, fragrant, solitary flowers are borne at or above the water surface on long stalks that are attached to the underground stems. Each cuplike flower has a spiral arrangement of its numerous petals."

Thirty-three years is the long stalk of the story of our marriage — from the beginning right up until now. The confessions are tropes. The monologue endures. The what-pushed-against and what-pushed-toward are the things we will not say, even to each other, the things that mark most every marriage, with minor-note adjustments. Thirty-three years, and ask me who I married, and I will say *him*. Artist. Architect. Salvadoran. A man whose country's colors are carmine, lemon, and lime, whose country's history is war and coffee, beauty and fear. A man whose hands can do anything, can do what other hands cannot.

Sometimes, here at the cottage at Lily Lake, my husband kayaks with me. Sometimes, in the two-seater pod, I kayak alone. Over the whispering forest of the lily pad stems, over the fragrant flowers, toward the opposite edge where the black bear live in the black shadows and the bald eagle has built a seven-foot nest. There are forty feet of depth beneath me and those creeping stems, the mud, and there's a blue heron that rests all its weight on a red-veined lily pad. It doesn't matter how far I go on the lake, because wherever I go, my husband is in the quiet near. He is on the dock casting, he is on the dock reeling, he is letting the bluegill and the pumpkin-seed and the black crappie go. He is slender, he is handsome, he is white-haired—an elegant man from a far-away country at a lake in the country I'm from.

Once a day while at the cottage of Lily Lake we take the Wrangler for a drive in search of lunch. The Jeep is old now, like us. It whines on the hills, talks out its troubles, refuses to fail. It delivers us to kielbasa or a sandwich or a salad, then back to the cottage, where I read and my husband fishes, or my husband fishes and I kayak, or I dock the kayak but my husband lifts it with his strength into its hold. All of this until it is time for dinner and we pour our cereal into the pretty bowls that we have borrowed from the cottage and drink our one glass of medium-fine wine.

There is a pattern of rain and a pattern of sun. There is wind through the pale pink pops. There is that yellow lily out among the whites in the skirt of lilies that floats near the dock. There is something I remember from an Eva Figes book I once read about Claude Monet and his planted pools: "He knew, though he could hardly make out their shapes, that the lilies would be closed tight as set pearls in the dark."

My biceps swell. Prettily.

"Happy anniversary," my husband says, on the morning of the day that is the actual day. I look up from Michael Ondaatje, whom I've been reading—"Is this how we discover the truth, evolve? By gathering together unconfirmed fragments?"—and say "Yes, happy anniversary," and my husband is slender and white-haired and handsome even now, and there's something slightly different in him, from yesterday, from the day before, and every day, if you pay attention to it, something is different. Every day of the thirty-three years.

Coffee. Cereal. The kayak together, the kayak lifted by his strength. Fish. A noontime trip in the Wrangler for soup and salad, and I'm back out on the lake and he's back out on the dock, and I wonder what we'll do here, on this lake, in my country, for our anniversary dinner. How we will celebrate the time together, except that we are together, and isn't that, shouldn't that, be the story? Our roots in the mud. Our lives still seeking light.

"We'll think of something," my husband says, has said, promised. He is a man who keeps his secrets, a man who can say nothing at all, much of the time, a man whose art speaks for him of the country he doesn't live in, the memories we don't share. A man of whom I have learned to ask small questions, only small ones.

The sun won't set until after eight. By half past five I'm in the only nice clothes I've brought with me to the lake. Our plan, my husband says, is to go somewhere for dinner with the one good bottle of wine, and I'm ready, he's ready, it's too early for dinner. "Let's go visit the lake," he says, and so we walk down the stone steps where the copperhead once lurked, under the popping pale pinks, past the fire pit, to the dock and lean our shadows over the baby bluegills and the white lilies, and the yellow one, worse for wear now, given the ministrations of the kayak. We take rare pictures of the two of us—catching ourselves in the wide-angle distortion of my phone; the sky grows out of our heads. We send the best one (there is not a good one) to our son.

Finally we return to the cottage, where all this time we have been alone but where now, it seems, we're not. There has been a knock at the front door, and I look to find a man in a salmon-colored shirt and a black-haired, blue-eyed girl with the kind of loose ponytail that suggests that she does not yet know her own beauty. She has a vase in her hands and it's stuffed full of flowers. He has a table-cloth, a candle, a basket of bread. He says his name and she says hers and then I ask her for her name again, because I am never good with names, and even after all these years with my husband, I am worse at surprises.

"She doesn't know," my husband says, about me.

"I hope you like bread," the man says. "It's warm. Homemade."

"Bill?" I say. My husband's name.

"Menus," the little girl says, and there it is, all written out, the particulate secret that my husband has been keeping: fig marma-lade, ancho chile puree, truffle cream sauce, pistachio crisp.

She sets the table, arranges napkins, remembers to serve from the right. She tells us that she sings, she knows every word of *Hamilton*. Her brother joins us, he's not yet six, he already cooks his family eggs three ways. The father goes up and down the hill, to the house that was built with muscle and imagination, where the chef, his wife, is working.

"How many years?" the man asks, and Bill answers, but I'm distracted by the delicate chives with their flower heads on, the red taste of the chile, the demeanor of the cheese, the mushrooms harvested from a forest in Montana, the grace and the goodness, and now I hear the man say, "Thirty-three years. Wow. How do you do it? What is the secret of your marriage?" and there has to be something to say, some wisdom, something to give back to this family that has built a cottage and a meal and a memory, this family that uses herbs as ribbons and flowers as tints and stuffs ravioli with the till of forest floors—an Uruguayan chef, we've now been told, and an American man and their invincibly appealing children, and so I offer what comes to mind: "We're both artists. We've learned to give each other room."

Is that right? Is that it? The answer to the question?

I want the chef to join us for dessert. I want all of them to come and sit with the meal and the wine, and to tell us how they made it and how they live here and what they might be looking forward to. "Stay," I say, when the chef at last arrives at the door—her dark ponytail as loose and signifying as her daughter's, and she does stay, and the others do, too, and suddenly the days alone in the cottage of Lily Lake are an evening of company on the occasion of a thirty-third.

We get to know each other.

We never know each other.

Stay. And then they leave.

"Thank you," I say to Bill.

Two words.

"Happy anniversary."

Two more.

Ondaatje, now, the next day, which is morning: "We order our lives with barely held stories."

It will be hot. Already the sun is a blade and we would go blind if we stared at the horizon, so we don't stare at the horizon; no marriage should. The lilies whisper beneath the pod of the kayak built for two, and then the fish jump and the bald eagle hides and no black bear emerges from the shadows, and I think of the five courses and the family, the way the solitary flowers are fragrant, they are showy, and I think of my husband, behind me, pushing against and pushing toward. I power forward and he steers, and we are at or above the surface of the water.

"What," I ask from my seat in the front where I can't see him, "is the secret of our marriage?"

Bill says nothing. The sun is a blade. I snag the stalks of the lilies with my dragonfly wings.

"I think it's that the longer you stay," he says, finally, "the more you will stay."

THE SHORT VERSION

He carried madcaps and misdemeanors forward, nearly fantastical triumphs of self-determination made heroic by the folktales they engendered. He would tame the wild mouse with stolen bread because he had been told *no mouse*. He would run the sewage tunnels because he'd been strictly warned against. He would invent the trespass, thrill the indiscretion, make his own choices, risk his own risks, seal friendships with the waxy pact of secrets. His childhood years were the years he would gladly live again, that he would always live, still. His memories were unsuppressed. They were exhilarating. He was laughing.

She felt the preponderant responsibility of her name, or maybe it was her middle-child status, or maybe it was the swell of ordinariness that she was quick to diagnose within herself. Why was she so quick? What had happened? It was hard enough to decide what she was—impossible to declare, with fixed assurance, her most enduring qualities. What she knew was that she tried to cage her secret wild parts. That she attempted fastidious obedience to the rules as she understood the rules to be. That she judged the world as harshly as she judged herself. That, once, she had found the baby bird in the strawberry patch—it was big-eyed, it was naked—and had brought it inside, to the warm soap smells of the laundry room, and that she had stood there unavailing as the bird tried to fly, and it could not fly, and it would not live, and she could not save it. That, once, she had rescued the cemetery stray, a green-eyed calico, and that she had wanted to rescue the calico kittens, too, born in an upstairs room, pink and alive but dead by morning. There was a kind of self-censorship that afflicted her heart, until the thoughtful little girl began to tell her little lies, and the white-socked child clawed into the soft-creek mud, and the self-negating teen unleashed a sharp, sarcastic tongue. The imperfection of trying to be perfect was the worst kind of imperfection there was.

And so they married.

THE LONGER VERSION

Salvadoran, Filipino, Spanish, Italian, and Pipil. His beauty was distracting, a lucky strike, a raucous impropriety, and love, in this case, had its antecedents on the eighth floor of the Headhouse Building in the offices of the Philadelphia architectural firm that employed them both. Him because of his actual architectural training and talent (and his friendship with the boss's son). Her because, as the great-niece of a famous architect and a student of language (or so she billed herself), she could be of some use to the firm's marketing efforts.

She had arrived first. He blew in like a category 3—charming, long-haired, and possibly dangerous, with news of a country split by civil war. He'd supported himself during a European year by singing in the streets. He owned a purple shirt, a reddish one, a pair of painter's pants, wooden clogs, a pair of tinted glasses. He smelled of smoke and linseed oil, excelled at volleyball, turned rectangles of thick, absorbent paper into surreal water-color scenes, and she wore pretty dresses and sensible shoes, and every day on her way to work she passed the crumbling walls of a nineteenth-century prison.

One day on that eighth floor of that Headhouse Building, three beautiful girls from his past appeared and—unjealous of each other—claimed him. They were easy with their looks, easy with themselves, easy with the gamble, and she watched, still brittle thin from the four solemn Ivy League years when she had whittled her flesh toward bones she saw as thick. She watched, an out-of-focus girl in pretty-enough pink and decent walking shoes. The boy and now those girls were category 3s, going up and down the halls and out to lunch and back and laughing, while the girl with decent shoes watched from her small kingdom among library books, binders, files.

One day the firm where they worked waged a battle with a rival on a softball pitch. He wasn't playing. She wasn't playing. She was watching him, watching his hands, listening to the fat ball struck by the hollow bat in the fading distance. She leaned a little closer to the stories that he told. El Salvador, a coffee farm, a war. Bob Dylan songs in a Roman tunnel. Near death thanks to a deal gone bad in the alleys of Morocco.

Everything foreign. Everything of interest. She wished to be of interest.

When he left the park and walked to the room he rented on a shady street, she walked with him, the sun going down beyond them. They climbed three flights of steps. He unlocked the door. He crossed the room to open the window and the sound of jump rope and late-day laundry swish came in. He showed her the watercolors he had left out to dry—arid landscapes walled in by ancient bricks. He showed her sketches, a battered guitar case. The linseed lived in a bottle where the drinks should be, and there was a mattress on the floor, Jethro Tull on cassette tapes, a drafting surface with a wired-in straight edge. When he sat in the room's one chair she sat with him, catching the breeze through the open window and listening to the swish.

She had abandoned all possibility of previous boys before she knew if she could love them. The kind Irish boy with freckles. The Mormon with intentions. The tennis playboy, ten years her senior, who fooled her mother with his talk of God and of religion. The boy who said he would jump from the roof of a college fraternity if she would not date him. His name was Gordon. She would not date him. She was loosely formed, with little knowledge of herself. She couldn't imagine who all those boys thought she was, and she wasn't wanting to be guessed at.

But after the softball game when neither he nor she played, after the click in the lock of the door in the room above Hamilton Street, she would return—watching him work, asking few questions, sometimes writing a poem of her own, sometimes dancing with the shadows on the wall, waiting, always waiting, as his wet water-colors swerved and buckled and ran, the colors ran. His paintings were raw and now it was their alliance that was the secret; no one they knew would know. They were a secret, and she wasn't sure why, but she assumed it was the plainness of the pink she sometimes wore.

Once, trying to open the door to that third-floor room, the key clicked and snapped in two. It was her fault; it was she who broke it; it was he who said, "We'll fix it." Once, hungry, she set out into the late night to a corner convenience store and ran, frightened, back to his room with a bottle of Coke, a bottle of ginger ale, a bag of chips, and he was still exactly as she'd left him, beautiful with color. Once she borrowed her father's car to take them to the sea, but when she rang the bell and rang the bell and rang the broken bell, he did not answer; it was days before she'd learn that he'd waited for her, wondered why she had never come. Once, packing his miserable white Civic, she said that she didn't believe that he'd remember her, for he was headed to New Haven, to his next adventure—graduate school for the watercolorist who was, as well, a profoundly good architect.

But he promised to write. But he said he would call. But mostly he did not. He was four hours north in a Brutalist tower on a green campus doing the things he deeply loved with friends who understood the vocabulary, geometry, risk of volumetric constructs. His happiness was innate and intact. His happiness was the smell of sepia and charcoal and the glue in the joints of the basswood models and late-night smoke and the hilarity of others who loved the childhoods that they had carried forward, who loved the stories he would tell.

She waited by the phone. The phone didn't ring.

She waited for letters. A watercolored postcard came—the beauty of its buckles tattooed by the machinery of postage.

In the room where she lived, in the neighborhood of the prison, a former tenant had hung a wide, wide mirror and left it there. She imagined a troupe of ballerinas on pointe shoes. She saw them in the mirror when she passed—thinner than she had starved herself to be, infinitely prettier in pink. She saw herself, too, so many versions. She saw herself, and she was waiting. She found another boy who would take her sledding in the snow. She let him kiss her. She let him say, *You are beautiful, You are smart, You are thin.* She let him be kind, even though she wasn't nearly so kind to him. And the snow fell and it fell and when next her unbroken doorbell rang it was the architect at the door, the fallen white in his hair, a gift in his hand—a book of blank pages and the pen with which she was to write her poems.

"Where have you been?" she said.

"I have been working," he said.

"You remembered," she said, "that I write poems."

Two months later she boarded a train to New Haven and found him in his room and said, "Yes. I will marry you," as if he had asked her, did he ask her? They did not divide their dreams; they did not name them. They did not say, *If this, then that, if this will be yours, this will be mine, these are our geographies, these will be our own apostrophes.* They did not say, *These are our childhoods—yours, mine—let us forgive them, let us forgive each other for what we do and what we can or can't carry forward.*

They just said *yes,* and she got on a train, and she returned to Philadelphia, and she rented another room so small that it would craze a small animal. She lived up to her name, which means House of God. He lived up to his name, which means Resolute. Two Junes from then they married.

She wore a discount dress.

He smelled of color.

PAYNES GRAY

I'd gone and fallen in love with the wrong man.

Said my mother.

She hadn't met him yet, but there were facts. He was Salvadoran (not my country), Catholic (not my religion), a subway-tunnel singer (I shouldn't have mentioned that), an architect who would rather be an artist.

(What sensible daughter marries a rather-be artist?)

And then there was the limit of his wealth: a beat-up Honda Civic that, last time I'd ridden in it, had seized to a halt in the longest stretch of the sketchiest part of town.

But his watercolors, I said.

His stories.

His art.

It was all there in his room in West Philly—laid out to dry. Fabulist landscapes on buckled Arches paper. Winsor & Newtons of ochre and dusk red. Oversized one-off postcards sending news of someone else's planet. I don't know which words to put down here first. How I saw his work, how it made me feel: craggy and leaning back and billowing with time.

When Bill left for graduate school he had no money for a phone and less time to write. He mailed me watercolors instead—washes of color in painfully occasional response to the voluminous ink bleed of my letters. When he returned two years later we built a life—my work on my pages, his work on his pages, a child soon enough, my mother in her eventual (and then steadfast) thrall of him. From poetry to fiction to essays to memoir to fiction to prose poems to categorical breaks for me. From paper to plaster to canvas to Kodachrome to the slick screen to the mud of the earth for him. And oxides. And stains.

There were years when I might have worried less.

Years when the demands of living exceeded the art of life.

Years that flurried on too fast.

But every time I saw my husband's art, I fell in love again.

Art is a tangle. Art is a mood. Art is the conversation you will or will not have, and there were more years and more art before the paintings and photos and sketches and smudges were not just drying in the near air or hanging on the sidewall or slouching in a black frame; they were tricking, twisting, wrangling their way into the stories that I tried to tell.

I wrote the wisdom of a garden but the memoir was more wise for having been relieved by Bill's photographs. I wrote a crooked little fable populated by crooked little creatures but everything was far more fabulously crooked, more distilled, more true, when Bill drew the characters to life. I wrestled with the line lengths of a poem that featured a hawk until Bill saw the hawk out there on the closest branch and took its photograph, then gave it to me, so that the shape of that bird might became the shape of my poem; it did. I wrote about truth and how truth gets made, but by then it was abundantly obvious to me: Bill's idiosyncratic drawings, his ghostly photographs, his rubbed-out sketches would make my point better, or make a different point, and now when I teach I bring Bill's art with me and spread it out across the table and say, to my students: "Five minutes, five sentences." Within the blink of that writing eye my students fabricate stories sprung from my husband's fantasies, his yearnings. The stories are theirs but they would never exist without this perfect stranger's art.

Some stories can be shaped by hand and others just cannot. Bill's colors are of the earth; I lean toward sky. His fabulism is credible; my realisms creak. Saturation is my drug, and trimming is his— take it away, pare it down, confront the final human hollow. We work different media with different hearts but the work is strengthened and abetted—my vision nicked and flecked by his, cracked and glued, called into doubt and argued back, and maybe, were he writing this, he would say something of the same about me. This, I think, is not just the condition of living with an artist; it is the artist's *essential* condition. To be startled, to be shattered, to be reinstructed, to be redirected, to seek out the thing you could not find yourself and then—by accepting, by contesting—to stumble straight past and then beyond your own constricting imagination.

You don't have to live with an artist to experience the shattering of another artist's vision. You only have to want the dialogue. You have to want to take the work of others as seriously as you take your own, value others as you value yourself, give time to extensions and tangents. You have to allow for different possibilities. You have to look for and then absorb that song, that canvas, that garden as if it were the thing you made, or the thing you might have made, or the thing that might teach you about what you are making. Five minutes. Five sentences. Find your true story in a perfect stranger's art.

Sometimes I watch my husband take a photograph. I stand in the light beside him, study the scene beyond him, watch him bend and snap, and still, later, will be undone by the slice of time he froze (how is it that I didn't quite see it?). Or I will tell him all that I know about a character I've written, and his resulting sketch will somehow be steeped with every indicating word, while resembling nothing that I've conjured. By thinking hard about how this artist sees, I learn more about my own seeing. I change the conversation that I am having not just with him, but with myself.

"Do you remember those old watercolors?" I asked Bill the other day. The first ones, the watercolors of West Philly? He went out to the shed where some of his work now gets done—on an easel, in a shadow box, in a kiln—and returned with a black portfolio that had been veiled by all these years of dust. He unzipped the thing, and there they were—the first fantasies as I remembered them, the witness of the hands I didn't resist, the names of the colors that sounded to me then like the strains of a subway guitar:

Alizarin crimson.

Paynes gray.

Purple madder.

Manganese blue.

WHY I NEVER LEARNED TO SPEAK MY HUSBAND'S LANGUAGE

Because I was a child lisper, ashamed to speak.

Because to speak another language, you must not be ashamed to speak.

Because to speak at all you must have dominion over your tongue and teeth, your rev and trill, and I had no dominion, I had no dominion, I had no dominion over me.

Because when I sat with the Spanish tapes in my American space, I could not *niño* nor *familia,* not out loud, not persuasively, for fear of the walls, which were not listening.

Because I was aware of all the mistakes I'd make, because he'd be aware, because pride got in the way, because he was already so much better than me at so many countable things.

Because if I spoke his language what would I say, who would I be?

Because I should have, because I did not, because our son did, easily.

DOUBLE PARENTHESES

In the dark underworld, Bill locks his elbows to his hips and pedals the wheel to mesmerizing speed. The mud fumes, geysers, drips. The jars of slip shift. Bill's torn jeans stiffen with the soft sweet earth, and later, after the pot on the wheel has grown leather hard, he takes a gentle knife to it.

Now he climbs the slant steps that lead from the dark to the light wearing the black snout and perforated pink disks of his particulate respirator. He smells of dry dust, webs, stained canvas, wet spouts. When he speaks, he sounds like an interviewee in the Witness Protection Program.

When he removes his mask the skin around his mouth is grooved by double parentheses.

Your work, meanwhile, is in eclipse. You're being undiscovered, unmade. You suspect yourself of having been a thief all along, of having never actually belonged. On the desks of editors. Inside the machinery of ink. On the published page. In the slight shadows of strangers' hands. There are bruises on your knees from your confessions. There is an ache in your heart, a cunning shame, and among the things you don't discuss are these:

The ideas that carry Bill into the slant dark
The invidious dangers of chemicals and flames
The frigid bucket water cracking the cells in his skin
The assertions over the made thing, the power of asserting
The indignity of retreat

Instead you just keep writing, slant. You write rogue. You write New Mexico. You write animal hurt. You write air. You favor a blueberry farm and a municipal airport and the rain through the pines of Ruidoso, and you believe in every word; you carve and trim and spin each word; you test and shift, you dig in with your own sharp stick, but again, the work encounters the world. Editors. Gatekeepers:

Given the author's sales record . . .
Given the mutations of the market . . .
Given the political socio book buying book selling disposition of
    the present hour . . .
Given the president . . .
Given the coming asphyxiation of the planet . . .

November, so many decades into us now, and the curators are on their way. Two men from an Old City shop who have found Bill's art, who have claimed it. You have swept and dusted and done the wife's work of small-charm hospitality, as bowl by spouted jar by vase by double-channeled vessel by twice-skinned pot, Bill delivers his kilned work to the dining room table. He warms the bowl of the chandelier with light. He waits.

You stand waiting, too. You stand remembering the room that Bill led you to, three floors high, when you were young. The smell of linseed. The pools of watercolor you dared to touch. The wobbly watercolor men with sepia bones. The hint of sawhorses and lead. The unframed bed. Yourself in that pink seersucker dress. Those ordinary shoes. The girls who hurricaned through while you stayed.

You, in your unfashionable pink, taped your poems to his walls.

You let your poem sounds run.

You wondered what it would be to marry a man for his hands. How long it would take for others to find him out for the beauty that he was. *Is.*

When the curators arrive, they are kinetic. Lit by the bowl of chandelier light, they cradle your husband's work with their effusing hands, open and close their hands, fill their hands, tilt the objects in their hands for an underneath look. They say *beautiful.* They say *rugged.* They say *story.* They say *yes* and *yes*, and Bill nods and you nod, and what they want is more.

In another room your name is running the spines of books. Your awards are slouching in frames. Your files are stuffed thick with yellowed newspaper claims. The bronze medal that, once, in a floor-length gown (velvet, the color of eggplant), you wore around your neck hangs limp around a frame. That ribbon nearly matched your dress. And that woman in the photograph is prettier than you'll be again. She looks like someone else. A doppelgänger of success.

December, and in the Old City shop, sales are brisk. A collector buys nine of Bill's pieces for her shelves in LA. A poet carries a vessel to her room. A sculptor of international repute chooses the prow of Bill's clay ship and prepares it for the long flight home.

More, the curators say. *More. Please.*

The bones of Bill's hands. The cracks in Bill's hands. The wedge, the slab, the spin, the trim, the carve of Bill's hands, the unshowy knowing of his hands. The trips he makes up and down the slant, cobwebbed steps and in and out of the city in his flap-windowed Jeep to the shop with the boxes of his things, where the curators are waiting.

Star ascendant.

More again. *Please.*

~🌼

You take a job, a corporate gig. You take another job. You teach. You write drug development stories, patient stories, community hero stories, TV scripts about artists on the rise and musicians who still sing. You interview writers in the high mist of being wanted, glitter their books, refer and guide, treasure and prize; and on your porch, outside, the books that now succeed pile and pile and want and want, say *more*, and now at night you dream yourself writing the stories you read and praise, the stories you love and teach, the stories your students are writing. You dream yourself immune to the future of your age, immune to the burying retreat.

You seek to be the blessing that you seek.

But no, the editors say. No to rain in the pines of New Mexico. No to the animal hurt. No to air itself, and to the sky, and to the first blueberry of the season. The truth thickens in you.

Bill photographs his baked pieces with a single peony. He photographs them with a stub of garlic, a twist of burlap, the hard red buds of grown things, a lemon, three brown eggs, a yellow pencil—because he doesn't know, he never knows now, if he will see these bowls, spouts, skins, again; if they will be permanently vanished from him, these wanted and alive things. The new, fresh clay has been dug from the earth of Spain, and it is so sweet, it is so desirably delicious, that when you touch it, you yearn to touch it more.

There are no words for how you love this man, for how your hopes for him have been achieved. You loved his talent first. You loved it more. You hope that he will not love you less, for all that you now are not.

You take a job. You take another job. You prize and you bespeak. You bow and shrink. You teach and you teach, you write for others, you write of others, you write (you cannot help it) slant, and you remember yourself in the pink seersucker dress. You remember yourself in the eggplant-colored gown. You feel harassed by the previous she; and maybe you will never sleep again, maybe you are too exhausted, now, to dream.

But you must sleep. You must claim possession of the couch in the room above the underworld, in the light that has grown dark. Beyond the glass door, the wind lifts the hem of pumpkin-colored leaves while beneath you the clay is on stampede. Whir and dip. Brush and stoke. Flame and crack. Made to hold. Made to be.

Last week, at night, while lying here because you have lost the perfect living thing, because you are not immune to anything, a raccoon lifted its paws to the lower panes of the door. You found the prints on the glass the next day and imagined yourself seen. You thought of the moon in its phases. You thought of the slow curve of your plots, and your gleam, and the purple on your knees.

A SHELTER FOR
THE TRUTH

What we do for each other is what there is. When he heats the water in my kettle. When I sweep his clay dust from the kitchen. When he tucks the corner of the bed. When I warm the croissants to their molten chocolate core. When I shovel the snow from the walk and he shovels the snow from the roof. When I choose the destination and he drives and I buy the tickets and he orders the lunch. When the blanket we share on the family room floor is faded, nubby, yellow, only warm when he lifts his arm and I fit my head onto his shoulder. When we ask what happens next, how long is next, how we will carry forward—he with his white hair now and fractured hands and waist 30 Levis and me with the eyes that blur the middle distance and the mind that, sometimes, wanders.

We are not heroic people; we won't be headlines. We might have been more than we made ourselves to be in the years of our living through the art that we forged, but we were persuaded by the consequences. The higher the climb, the more dire the fall. The greater the wealth, the more formidable the spend. The more you seed a public need for yourself, the less time you spend at home. No one is exalted always. No one is perpetually esteemed. No one is in implacable demand. Those who get everything end up wanting something different, and we have learned enough, Bill and I, to know not to want too hard, not to exploit our moments, not to lose sight of what a good life serves.

Still, the river flows, we need a raft, we need to build the raft. He with his hands and me with my stories and us with our wish for more in this tumble of time until one becomes a burden for the other, or we become a burden to our son.

"I've chosen my bridge," Bill will say, or "Two through the head," or, "Amsterdam. Switzerland. Oregon." It makes me angry when he says it, shuddered through with excessive responsibility and withering loneliness and the knowledge that we are the same in this, watching the clock, affrighted not by the certainty of death but the uncertainty of what precedes it.

Years from now, a perfect stranger's story will somehow feel as my own, a future telegraphed:

"'Sue decided that she strongly wished not to descend into dementia under indefinite institutional care,' Brian Hubbell said by email. 'So, on the morning of Sunday, Sept. 9, she ate her last grapefruit and informed her friends and doctor that she intended to stop eating and drinking. She stuck to her plan and died 34 days later, increasingly lucid through the last few days.'"

In her final conversations with him, he added, she said she considered the ending to her life that she had orchestrated "a triumph." (New York Times obituary, Sue Hubbell)

It is 2016, and the news of the world is bad news. The man who will too soon be in charge of executive orders and public discourse is a triumphant liar. In the classroom at the university where I teach, home is our centralizing theme, and George Hodgman, Annie Dillard, and Ta-Nehisi Coates are our guides, and when I stand in the borrowed Victorian manse asking the students, "What is truth and why does it matter?" the answer is never the same. The truth is never fixed, the truth is elusive, the truth is a betrayal, the truth can be boring, and it matters, and we reckon, and at home we reckon, and on Tuesdays I walk the distance and take the train and cut through one campus toward another, then stand again among the students, exhorting and provoking and extending, calling anecdote out for what it is, sending the students out onto the street with cameras, asking for honest self-assessments. Are you a plain-prose writer or a fine writer? Are your words summer or winter? What details, now, do you see? I recall what George Hodgman, writer of compassion, author of *Bettyville*, said, on the rainy day when he Skyped in to Penn from his home in St. Louis, Missouri.

"The worst books are the perfect books," he said. "The worst books are the ones that feel safe."

We'll build a workshop, we say. And it isn't safe, it can't be safe, we tell my father. He shakes his head. He pencils numbers onto a pad. "That is no way," he says, "to make a living."

It might be a way to live.

We start. Bill scouts and brands and files and webs; he banks. I buy six three-inch binders and multicolor folders and pull every memoir and near memoir that I own onto the floor and think: five-day workshops, five days of curriculum, ten hours a day. A sense of purpose. A kind of community. An art that speaks of and for the heart. It will matter because we'll make it matter. It will change lives, not just our own. It will be a decent raft. A raft intent on decency. No fame. No fortune. Just the conjunction of us. Our Juncture.

There are cabins by a lake, Bill says. There is a pueblo in a town. There is a working farm. There are chef's tables. One of them or none of them will be the place where this begins.

"What do you think?" Bill asks.

"What do *I* think?"

I think I have never seen my husband look like this before. I think that marriage, a long marriage, cannot allow itself to grow old. I think that love is anything but indifference.

I think of the magic shows of my childhood—my brother and me at a puckered card table, tricks up our sleeves: nickel per show. I think of lemonade stands: quarter a glass. I think of the beaded rings I made when I was a kid—a nickel or a dime for some custom ring work, a dollar for a bracelet.

"I'll make some calls," Bill says.

Bill has a hunch about 175 acres of a working farm in Central Pennsylvania. Piglets, peacocks, barley, corn, a fishing pond, Civil War traces, a big barn and a series of cottages set down on an inner loop road that are rented to dreamers and wayfarers like us. The Juncture boardroom is our own small kitchen. The Juncture conference table steams with Bill's coffee. The Juncture dress code is pajama casual.

On one end of the table the folded laundry sits, emitting laundry smells. Bill presents his case, my iPad in his hand. Writers need quiet, he says. Subtract the brays, moos, and bird calls, and the farm is quiet. Writers need inspiration. The farm is pastures, mountains, sky. Writers need stories. The farm is thick with them. The cottages, Bill says, are resurrected structures that have been trucked down county roads—summer kitchens, a corn crib, a pig's sty, a used-car-lot office that was twice displaced and transposed before being reborn as a bedroom plus bathroom/kitchen. There are four hundred families in this borough. There is a train depot forty minutes away. Bill has called the owner. He has trusted her voice. It's worth looking into, he says.

The laundry cools.

We settle on a February visit to the farm. We head north and west, in ice-block weather, the old blue car with the wrong-wheel drive chugging off the miles. We're not an hour away from home before the landscape eases and the frozen farms quilt off in all directions. Two hours, and there are cliff walls, river gorges, elevated views of isolated living. Every now and then we stop to see what is happening out here—the sudden smash of sunlight on a cupola, the silvering of a river, the blue silo stacks with their hopeful ladders.

We are through the town before we see it. We stop, turn around, track back, park before the only public building we find: the post office. Bill hurries through the cold, opens the door, reappears with a word about nearby restaurants. There is one, he says, a diner up the road. I've never been so glad for a sandwich.

Back on the road, we are, in fact, the only ones out on the road. Our satellite signals fade. I type a quick text to our son: *Going under*. Ulsh Gap Road Ts into Back Mountain Road, and there, in the near distance, it is. The farm that Bill has found. A plank in our raft, or is it the twine, or maybe it's a flag.

There are skirted evergreens along the entrance road. The road is narrow, icy, long. Bill slows the car and we take in the view—the woman in the distance, the white worms of wrapped hay, the long fences and metal silos, the snow that gets whipped up with the wind, passing a veil across the backdrop hills. When we reach the farmhouse, Bill slows again. The car's wheels jump then slide, and as Bill tries to right the car, to stop it from its angled glide, the woman begins running, waving hello, disappearing and returning with a bag of sticky salt. She tosses the salt to the ground as if she's sowing wildflowers. We regain our traction and she runs, now, ahead of the car, leading us on our way to the Yetter, the little yellow house where, on this evening, we will stay. We are the farm's only guests. We step away from the cats. The cats are back at our ankles. Their tails are a brush of warmth.

We leave our one bag in the room and walk the inner road past the stables, toward the big barn where the farmers live. It is a building of put-together parts, small in the alcove where all the muddy boots sit, big in all other places. Sally leads us to the piece in this puzzle where the sun falls in. To a museum of things hung from hooks on the walls, the rafters, the fixtures—Conestoga wagons, wheel parts, oil horns, detached spiral stairs, tins, signs, antique rifles, barrels, buckets, tools, so many things that I begin to doubt that there are only three dimensions.

"My husband," Sally explains, "is an historian."

Sally is practical, handsome. After years of working, rebuilding, sustaining a farm, nothing, I suspect, can surprise her. She has gathered calves, raccoons, porcupine quills, kittens, peacocks, eggs, rainfall, crops that came in too soon or barely. She has transformed a used car sale office, a pig's sty, and a lean-to into tiny houses with discrete views. She has raised her children, played her part in the September county fair. She watches Bill as he talks, as he paints this picture of this thing we want, this thing we have gotten into our heads to do. Workshops, he is saying. Communities of twelve. Landscapes that provoke. Something different. Something for now to compensate for then. Something to keep us near to each other.

Sally knows something about near. We talk. She knows something about teaching. She taught before she farmed. She tells stories, now, about the seasons of the farm. About her daughter's cooking. About a photographer friend who has brought photographers here, hosted them like we will host our writers. A congregation has turned this farm into a camp. Weddings have been held out in the barn by the hills. Communities have happened at this T in a long road.

Bill has a checklist. Sally has answers. She'll work with us, give us leeway. She suggests a week in September. The sun moves. The bicker and bray of the animals beyond us push up against the glass, and Sally stands, invites us on a tour. "You'll see what you think," she says. "*Really* think." We find our boots beneath the paws of resting kittens. The air outside is arctic. The interior road is frozen, slick.

We follow Sally from cabin to cabin—across porches, into winter-ized rooms, up hand-built stairs, back down into the stillness of frozen kitchens. The mattresses have been stripped. The windows have been curtained. No one has occupied these rooms since summer. I extrapolate the season, imagine September light. Doors open. Chairs rocking. Vases with a spill of flowers. Writers at their tables, writing. The past lives of these cabins seeping into the work that might get done.

Soon Bill and I are on our own. We retrieve our cameras from the former car-lot office. We go off in our own directions, giving each other room to frame this story as we individually see it, this possibility. The one russet horse in the white barn has my attention, comes close, allows me to touch the stripe on his head with my glove, to take a portrait of the dark mane that falls like long bangs around his eyes. The peacocks and the peafowls are in an uproar behind him, bobbing the feathery crowns on their heads, rustling their iridescence, bothering the black rooster with the collar of gray, the white hens with the orange masks, pecking at the antique signs, hiding in truck beds. The cows are at full graze in their pens. The pigs are masticating cobs. There is a silo of a cage where feathered things are kept out of the reach of the raccoons.

Trucks are frozen into the rutted road. The pond is frozen. The white worms of hay are frozen. I walk the narrow road toward the gallery of skirted trees and then walk back, zooming the lens so that the mountains come into view, then the silos, then the big farmhouse, where the lights are on, the hacksaws hung like lanterns on an old tool shed, a skull on top of a ribbed barrel, the molars crooked in that head. I can barely breathe with the cold. The sun has started to ratchet down the sky, turning the ice on the road into gold. I run, I slip, I run back to the yellow cabin. Two cats are on the porch like sentries. Bill is already in, blowing warmth into his hands.

"What do you think?" he asks.

I think, I think, that I want every minute I have left with you.

On a suburban campus not far from our home, I teach, again, a single immersive week. In a room with six others, I dissolve into the nearly invisible seventh. They are dark-haired, electric-haired,

I had a young son, we had a porch of our own, I was there. I *am* there—dark-haired, elastically skinned, unknown, unheralded, just a young writer writing a story about buttons. I am there, and my son zooms a miniature car down a plank highway, he hums himself a song, he cannot know what he will become, he doesn't have the words, yet, for his stories, while on the opposite end of a long train track my husband works a job he doesn't love, and he is wasting time, wasting life—he is a foreign man who is not happy in my America, this cannot last. I cannot make the time come back in the story I am writing. I cannot turn that time into something else.

I cannot fix what's lost.

The next day I tell the writers to strike the empty. Untangle. Decompress. You have written a song but you have misplaced a verse, I say. Explain little. Evoke all. Begin with the road you were driving on, then describe the lace. Exploit the window. Know the question you are writing to. Don't force the answer.

Now I ask them to make a list of the strengths they have discovered in their writing.

"I communicate tenderness," one says.

"I trust the reader."

"I like lists."

"I evoke emotion."

"I use sharp, cutting words."

"I create visual spaces."

"I am a storyteller."

"I understand the purpose of prologue."

I study their faces. It is our last day. I vow to remember them, to honor them. The girl with the electric hair has a question. "What if," she says, "you built a house of memoir? Could you," she says, "do that?"

I drive into a sunset with the car windows down. I snap the apocryphal world news to silence.

The grace in you, they had said, one to the other.

The power of your forgiveness.

You have found your story. There.

Your greatest achievement is not behind you.

A house of memoir, she said. A shelter for the truth.

When I arrive home, the news is on. Bright flares of it in the lenses of Bill's glasses. He lies on the floor, those two round pillows at his head. I sit on the couch above him, hover. Neither of us speak. The news is bad: angry, random, inconsolate. The news is in the order Lester Holt and his team of intrepids offer. When, after some time, I ask Bill a neutral, non-news question, when I try to make space for the house of memoir, the shelter for truth, the affirmation of our dream, Bill diverts by telling me that he had not wanted to drive far for lunch today. I don't realize, at first, that this seeming insignificance is prelude. That what Bill means to say, that what he is saying now, is that earlier in the day, returning from the gym, a van ran a red light. A van was speeding down a hill and Bill was in his Jeep, waiting to make a left-hand turn, trapped in the traffic fist of an intersection, and a van ran the light. A van came, zooming.

"It was close," Bill says. "It was very close. I didn't want to drive far after that."

I reach. I touch his soft, white, dear head.

Your greatest achievement is not behind you.

A heat dome squats above this slice of earth, fire ashes the west, floods vanish Southern streets, tornadoes chow through Midwestern roofs, and the news is bad. Hate as a plan, revenge as a politics, armed madness, coups. Orlando, Turkey, Bangladesh, Dallas, Nice, Turkey again, Baton Rouge, and now the first day of a political convention in a city mauled by fences, open firearms, war-sized police battalions to keep the predicted protestors back, and a presidential candidate in gleeful pursuit of divisions. The birds go lazy beneath the weight of the heat, and the cicadas are in chaos.

Upstairs, in our son's room, Bill is working the ancient computer keyboard with two fingers—his hair high on his head, his feet bare. Behind him, Raggedy Andy, Donald Duck, Macaroni, and Jeremy the Frog sit wedged together on a stuffed-animal-sized bench, stadium seating. Three empty suitcases block the attic door. An old game of Shoot the Moon has dropped the silver ball. An orange tiger on squeaking wheels could use a nap. The desk itself is tenement of surfaces—books upon books, a cup of pennies, a bowl of nickels, *The Art of Looking Sideways*, a plaster replica of the Triangle Building, two sets of headphones, an untapped Crate and Barrel card.

Look, I say, bringing him the mail. Application envelopes for our inaugural workshop. One is thick with confetti. One is flocked with purple flowers. One is tied together with bits of orange ribbon and green string. And in every envelope that comes to us, that waits like a white fish in the dark slip of the P.O. box, there is a wide remembered kitchen, for that is the single thing that I have asked of the writers who might join us: Tell me about a kitchen.

A Reynolds Oven Bag. That's the secret to a juicy turkey. My mom didn't teach me that. I discovered it on my own. Wrote Annie.

It's just a steak, I told myself. Wrote Karen.

I begin the chopping. Wrote Lynn.

"What do you think?" I say.

There are parts of me in the reflection of his glasses.

An impeccably ugly rented Chrysler will float us forward. Bill pops the trunk and the big gray maw of the thing takes our propositions in. The three-ring binder with its rainbow-colored plastic sleeves bearing the imagined order of the teaching days, the lecture notes, the excerpts: *The Art of Home. The Art of Portraiture. The Art of Time and Place. The Art of Context and Uncertainty. The Art of the Prologue.* The beat-up, underscored, written-over copies of *Lab Girl* (Hope Jahren) and *Violation* (Sallie Tisdale). The bottles of wine (there might have been more red, we will learn, than white). The bottles of water (how innocent we still are about how essential this will become). The cookies I've baked, the insufficient coffee and the excessive tea and the yellow bag of sugar and the multiple flash-lights, the projector my father has donated to the cause and the laptop that will die one single day post-workshop. The eleven vases that Bill has shaped and the kiln has bisqued and I have glazed in combinations of Yellow Salt and Wildflower Speckle, Ohata Khaki and House Shino, Sweet Cream and Weathered Bronze. The eleven Field Notes T-shirts Bill has designed based on his concept of a writer, a concept it seems I have inspired. The T-shirt design suggests a packing label, complete with a bar code and warning signs: *Fragile. Flammable. Not Edible. Not to be submerged or dropped or disturbed.* Then this disclaimer:

All writers are exquisitely handmade, one at a time, using natural products. It is therefore quite difficult, if not impossible, to make them identical. Color, dimensions, and finish may vary. Naturally occurring blemishes make each writer charming and unique.

We're in motion. I feel the weight in the trunk slide to the left then to the right as Bill pulls the Chrysler into the highway's slow lane. West. He watches for signs of trouble. I watch him, discreet, my seat pushed back. He is the beauty between us, framed now by the world beyond—the exurbia becoming farmland, the silver verticals of silos, the quick flick of cow tails. His face is distinct against the blur—the angles of his jaw, chin, and cheek, the ink spots of his freckles, his eyes behind the rectangle of his glasses, a Sia song playing through him.

The Chrysler drags to the left; Bill commandeers. Sia sings another song and agriculture singes. Bill's eyes on the road, my eyes on him, and this is our certain thing because nothing, now, is certain.

Once I wrote a memoir about my marriage. The pages braiding El Salvador, landscape, civil war, coffee, Spanish, us. The writing was a journey toward understanding this: How well do we ever really know those we come to love? The hope was to halve the distance between lovers, to reckon with the power of strange and foreign things, to honor the mystique of the unknown. Fifteen years it took to write that book, and when it was done it became an instant artifact, for there were still so many things I had not named, had not reckoned with, still so many ways I could not reach this man I loved, still so many times that I was stopped by the contradictions between us, the unhalved distance. His calm and my intensity. His exotic past and my suburban one. All that he can make with his hands and all that I cannot. The way he talks and sometimes doesn't. The way I don't talk, then do. How he doesn't grow old. How I always grow old. How we are always growing old.

"Why do you love me?" I have asked him, repeatedly.

He will not answer. He is still here.

"What did we forget?" he asks now, over the Sia.

"Nothing that matters," I tell him.

Drought has come to this September. Beyond Bill, the Juniata River runs thin, its exposed rocks like the fossil bones of a theropod. The houses on the lower lip of the highway seem weakened by undiluted sun, and once we reach the narrow roads of Snyder County, the colors of the quilted farms run to sorrel, fawn, the occasional startling green. The corn has been buzz cut down to its dry nubs. The cows lift and slap those paintbrush tails. Abandoned wheels and hex signs lean against the shingled bottoms of crowded sheds. Maybe not abandoned. Maybe found.

We stop just west of Middleburg, off Route 522, at a greenhouse/ garden center called Engle's. We are in search of cut flowers to fill the empty vases in the Chrysler maw, but what we find here instead is an emporium of potted, plantable things—fruit trees, bright vines, mums, roses, hanging baskets all set out in open-air groves and parabolic nurseries. We walk nursery to nursery, each parabola growing more and more sparse until our shoes echo with every step and I take Bill into my arms, whisper to him, invite him to dance. "No one is looking," I say, and no one is, but now we hear a pattering above our heads, see the blots of rain on the glass roofs, step out of the nursery and look toward the groves and watch as this sudden rain falls. The show lasts five minutes. Then the rain is gone. A localized tease of silver and glisten.

Back in the car we head toward this place called McClure and its few hundred people, the rudiments of the McClure Bean Soup Festival and Fair, now in its 125th year, down the hill from us, at the edge of town. The amusements, eateries, exhibition halls sit nearly empty, waiting for the crowds we'll never find, the coming days of prize-hoping pickles and jarred white cherries, Little Miss Bean, Teeny Bean, the Milk Chug and the Shoe Box Float contests. The road we are driving swoops up, then down, and then we turn onto Ulsh Gap Road, another high and low of curves and bends. We do not pass, for a little while, the horse-drawn carriage managed by a straw-haired boy.

When Ulsh Gap Ts into Back Mountain Road, we keep driving, straight on in toward the blue-green hills. What was ice in winter is now a gravel road. White dust rises toward the arch of big-skirted trees. The cows, the pigs, the peacocks, the herder dog, the cats of February are here. The eye of the pond is closed beneath a lid of algae.

Sally is brooming down the wooden picnic tables when we find her. We bring her reports of the sudden rain, the lone crack of lightning between the nurseries and here. But the rain has skipped her slice of earth, she says. Weeks now, she says, without a meaningful drop, worst drought since 1976, and the cistern on this spring-fed farm is sinking, she reports, toward dry. The tap water is not to be trusted. There are bottles of water in each room. As we stand there talking there is a tease of moisture, no more than two minutes of hardly any rain. That would be a rainbow above our heads, Sally tells us. But we're standing too close to see it, and it won't be until we almost leave that we'll learn how close Sally had actually come to calling off the workshop for lack of rain.

Of all the things that might have capsized us, we never thought of weather.

The cabin where we will stay is a former carriage house that once lived creekside down the road. It has been dragged here, along with the carriage wheels, the barrels, the Civil War rifles, the signs, the stoves, the bell jars, the oil horns, the frames of Conestoga wagons, the other cabins and their couches, by a family, a community who cannot waste a thing. In this modernized version of a nineteenth-century space, a black spiral stair connects the great room to a loft, two bedrooms wait behind a glass door, and an antique coffee maker hunkers down in the kitchen. Two fabric-faced dolls guard a Danielle Steele novel, while, on a table outside, an alabaster peahen cocks her head to spy on us.

We unburden the Chrysler. We fill the vases with the silver leaves we finally bought at Engle's. We daisy chain the sofas and the chairs into a great room circle, put the coffee in the kitchen, the bottle opener. It is three thirty in the afternoon, twenty-four hours until the writers arrive. We text messages to our son, but a cell tower is down, and our words echo back at us.

As the sun starts to sink, we drive the gravel road to its end, hook into Ulsh Gap, turn right toward Lewistown. On either side of the road sit the big and little houses, the pickup trucks and abandoned motors, lives behind thick curtains. The sky is purple. The clouds are white balloons.

In Lewistown, Zion, the hair salon, is closed. The movie theater's open, but it's empty. A cardboard statue of Donald Trump shoulders out an entire storefront, and down the middle of the street, beyond the courthouse and the Civil War mementos, a man skateboards past, oblivious to us, the only other people on the street.

We find an open restaurant and two tall stools, ribs and rotisserie chicken. I worry the cistern, the earth, the eleven almost on their way. I worry us, this far gone in this direction. I worry worrying Bill, and now there is no one on the streets when we leave. No car but ours in the lot. We drive through town in the dark, Bill fiddling with dials, until he stops, lost now and without headlights, in a narrow alley. By the glow of my phone, the headlights knob is found. We weave around the edge of town until we're back where we belong, fifty miles per hour beneath the spotlight of the moon.

That night not even a whole pink pill kills my insomnia. I lie beside Bill listening to squawkers, conjuring bears on the blue-green hills and a bracelet of snakes in the trees and rust in the bottom of the cistern. My heart is a black bird perched on a thin limb that startles quick, ferociously, and now I feel my way out of the room, down the short hall, through the glass door, toward the daisy chain of sofas and chairs, where the floor is cold against my bare feet and it is too dark to read the shadows.

Everything in that white notebook in those rainbow sleeves is theory. Everything I teach will necessarily bend to the coming writers' stories, the palpable and the prismatic, the squall of what they want from words, their willingness to sit right here, on Goldilocks chairs, and address the tumult of language and life. *What is memoir?* I will ask, and their answers will mark our true beginning, reconstitute any plan I have, reshape the story of my marriage.

Memoir is the adapted and adaptive truth. Teaching memoir is a negotiation. My feet cold, the dark relentless, I cross back toward the bedroom wing and turn not left, where Bill is sleeping, but right. Hands out before me, tiny steps, I feel my way toward the empty bed. Pull down the quilt. Pull it up, to my chin. Wait for dawn.

"What do you think?" Bill says, when he finds me in the morning.

"I think it's time," I say. And kiss him.

In the morning the geese and the peacocks are out by the dock, watching the open eye of the pond. The bearded goats won't leave their barn. The russet cows stand on mounds of hay as if on lookout, the horse holds its own among a barnyard of peculiar things, a chicken plans to lay its green egg in the cab of Sally's truck, and at the end of the gravel road, the sunflowers lift their heads to this day's sun. Piglets the size of house cats storm the stalks, their wrinkled snouts and Spirograph tails only sometimes visible in the caper.

It's Sunday in McClure, church bells and carriages, and I'm still wide awake. At Hillside Market two miles southeast, neighbors talk weather around a speckled countertop and the market shelves offer goods in ones and twos. One bottle of aspirin. Two boxes of Hamburger Helper. One tube of toothpaste. One container of bleach.

Enough of everything for now.

The first writer arrives just after three. Bill and I have been waiting
for her on the farmhouse stoop, by the buzz of flies near fallen fruit.
The peacocks scatter, the old hen, the freckled guinea fowl, and
there Annie is, in the passenger's side, waving a two-armed hello,
her wife at the wheel. I tell them to follow me, and I run while
they drive past the broomed tables and the lazy eye of the pond
to Annie's cabin, where a vase waits by her bed and the T-shirt
plumps her pillow. The frames of her glasses are a dazzler's blue,
her eyes are a dazzle, her style is sweet stagger.

"You're here," I say.

She is.

For the next three hours, it will go like this: the fruit-drunk flies, the
white lift of dust, the rumble of tires, the disturbance of feathers as
Roxie, the prime pup, herds the writers in—Lynn with a streak of
purple in her hair, Toby with her red lipstick style, Tam with the
perfect tattoo, Hannah straight from a bridal shower, Jessica with
a spark of a heart, Tracey with her contagious laugh, Karen with
her Texan grace, Starr who looks precisely like her name, and I run
them from cabin to cabin, dust in my shoes now, dust in my hair,
all that has been imagined displaced by a new, incumbent real.

By six, Sally has laid the lace down over two adjoining tables in
the big barn's great room and set the family-style down—cubed
watermelon, roasted beets, sliced turkey, zucchini casserole, a
bowl of pear tomatoes—proof of what the earth still yields, of
what is possible. In the passing of dishes, in the start of talk, in the
quieting that comes when Sally's husband speaks of the history
here, the auctioneer's obsessions, the rescue and salvage of things,
I reach for Bill's hand. An hour from now the writers will tell me

what memoir is—*an attempt to hold onto memory, the story of the way we choose to see the truth, the journey of recalling the journey*—but right now we are simply here, so many streams of rare liquid earth converging.

Over the next many days, the sun will break through a blue mist, the piglets will storm the stalks, Roxie will chase the balloons of clouds, the cats will skein, the chicken will lay its green egg in the cab of that truck, the peacocks will drop their feathers, and in Sally's house, on Sally's porch, in the daisy chain of chairs and sofas, we will find ourselves and our stories. We will read of Dawn Raffel's childhood rocking chair and decode our own generative, remembered things—that blue eye in a box, that mahogany breakfront, that green crockpot. We will read stories built out of single rooms and lay our own foundations. We will write community and, to counter that, we'll listen to the lonely of Olivia Laing:

Imagine standing by a window at night, on the sixth or seventeenth or forty-third floor of a building. The city reveals itself as a set of cells, a hundred thousand windows, some darkened and some flooded with green or white or golden light. Inside, strangers swim to and fro, attending to the business of their private hours. You can see them, but you can't reach them, and so this commonplace urban phenomenon, available in any city of the world on any night, conveys to even the most social a tremor of loneliness, its uneasy combination of separation and exposure.

We will learn portraiture from Hope Jahren. Landscape from Hisham Matar. The return to the past from Rebecca Mead. Summer from Terrence des Pres. The continuum of time from Sallie Tisdale: "We talk about the wheat going in tomorrow. We talk about the little maple tree, still alive. We don't talk about how our lives are fettered one to the other in the perfumed soil of the spring. Then, I didn't even know that much." In the morning hours, in the afternoon, in the evening dark, we will write, listen, ask ourselves, about the work we hear: What confuses? What astonishes? What will be remembered? What is the perspective? What is the story here?

Saturate, I will tell them. Abandon thin reporting. Get out of the way of your story. That dog does not belong there. Find at least two true stories and braid them and listen for the reverb in between them because maybe that reverb is your story. And when they read aloud the room is hush. When they tell their stories, everyone listens. When their time is their own, I find them together—twos of them or threes or fours—running Ulsh Gap past the straw-haired boy, leaning forward on their cabin porches, laughing until they have to stop inside their idiosyncratic rooms.

All this time, Sally walks the hill behind, checking on the health of the spring, measuring the water the roots of the trees have released back into the earth in the cooler dawn. She studies old *Farm Journal* cookbooks, harvests, with her daughter, the hot earth's yield, stirs into pots that have cooked this family's meals since her wedding day. The strain of the drought wears on her, the forty-four head of cattle and their too-crisp hay, the piglets in the rustling stalks, the tomatoes that ripen into hollow versions of their natural selves, that green lid on the eye of the pond, the brown wither of tall trees. We watch her, we watch the skies, we hope the clouds toward a steadfast place, and the landscape enters our vocabulary; we write of drought and yield, waiting rooms, the ghosts of misplaced things, things not lost yet.

On Wednesday afternoon, Bill connects the dying laptop to my father's old projector, borrows a makeshift screen from the cabin, flips a chair to its side and places it on the picnic table, and delivers theater. Bill's own photos fill the screen. He moves image by image through pictures stolen from time—his time, ours. He suggests. He names strategies. The rule of thirds. Natural frames. Unexpected croppings. Surprising points of view.

Sitting on the back of the couch, the spiral of the steps, a picnic bench, the writers watch, listen, and I watch, too, this man whom I have stood beside for more than thirty years, listening to his camera snap, gauging his perspective. But here, in this moment, with the skies darkening beyond us, I see Bill as someone new. I see him as these women do, as someone still apart from me, as someone I will fall in love with again, doesn't matter that he already has my heart. I accept his theories. I write his answers to the questions I have never asked him. He has tilted his camera like this because. He has sunk the ribbon of a road beneath a massive sky because. He has pushed the sailor off center because. He has pursued the diagonal because.

He is done. He hands each writer a piece of folded paper, and on each fold of paper there is a phrase: Mood. Texture/Pattern. Routines. Geometric Shapes. Light/Shadow. Tools/Machines. Buildings/Details. Vessel/Container. Patterns. Animals. Weather/ Atmosphere. He asks the writers to spend the remainder of the day as photographers—to go out into the afternoon alone with their cameras. What they frame in their viewfinder, what they snap and snatch, will teach them something more about who they are and what they are capable of, how they see.

Tiny spits of rain fall, then stop falling.

The afternoon remains gray.

I shadow the writers, quiet, behind them. Watch them look. And see. And take. A calm settles in across the farm. Stories minus words. A wasp and wrinkled leaves. A spider's net in rusted chains. An empty walnut shell. Abandoned boots by a rocking chair. The skittishness of feathers. A bent lantern. A round knob on a rectangle door. The weave of strings. Sally's hands in water. That little bit of rain on the sleepy-eyed pond. Roxie on the road to something. A stack of mattresses in an uphill room. Cows in the far distance. A broken wreath of onions. A long white worm of wrapped hay. The machinery of teeth in a gray skull's jaw.

It is active. It is entirely still. The skies bruise, but the rain begs off. I see Hannah, in the distance, a pink umbrella blown inside out like a pretty skirt in one hand, her other hand tossing a leaf to the wind: atmosphere. I see Tam shooting the empty between tree limbs. I see Toby crouching down. I see Karen looking up, not sure. To what they find, to how they see, the writers grow intimate, close. Tomorrow, they will find inside the pictures they have taken, their own transformative metaphors. Their stories will be even more true for having looked, in this afternoon, beyond themselves.

On Friday, we meet again for the last time. We gather in that daisy chain of hard and soft to hear the prologues that have come to be, the vessels these writers will carry home, these containers of voice, mood, story. I take my place in that hard chair. I thank the writers for being there—for coming in the first place, for remaining. And now our Starr begins to read, and suddenly, like the long tail of a white cat, her truest story swooshes into view—a city's legacy, a personal myth, a mother, brightly seen, a writer's beginning. She reads, and I cannot speak. My tears run hard. I lift my wet eyes to find hers. "Really?" Starr says, when she is done. "Really," I whisper. Because her work is that good. Because she has traveled this far. Because she is here, with us—strangers no longer strangers. Strangers on a raft.

Memoir is the life wanting to be transformed. It is the life we have been waiting for.

One hundred forty-nine miles to home, and Bill is at the wheel of the rented Chrysler. The world beyond rushes on—the dry quilts of the farms, the up-thrusting silos, the paintbrush tails—but Bill is entirely specific. Bill has made this thing even more than I have made this thing because he pressed me, pushed me, to know myself irrefutably, to claim something that seems so small on the scale of things, but is so big to me. To us.

Our slantwise faith in good, small things.

We choose as our own the house with a wide porch and blue-striped pillows on the wicker chairs, say, where marigolds grow in pots and mint in window boxes and a black cat nudges the edge of a stair with its chin.

We claim the shed in the back for the throwing of Bill's clay. We claim the front window as my writing lookout. We claim the basil in the pots. We agree that we are expertly well put in this spot, three blocks, as it is, from the heart of this town. We love the distance we have sketched from trouble. We love our neighbor's ingenuity. We love the smell of the smoked wood on the grill.

We agree that water gives a town weight, that the sea is atmospheric. We need water. Or we agree on the need for turquoise vistas and sand, the spirit of Georgia O'Keeffe, the ghost of Willa Cather, the food at the inn. Or we agree on the mystery of dried-out river-beds, the dent that they might make in our imaginations. We agree that a town depends upon excellent coffee and also good tea, moist baked things, at least three restaurants, a place that sells heirloom tomatoes, mint in lemonade, proximity to friends. We agree that we are not finished yet. That the river water runs. That our raft is holding.

Eventually we head back toward the Tudor. The road rumbles beneath us, the wide stripes of wheat stretch out beyond us, the signs stand out before us. We exit, turn. The big roads become small ones. The familiar things are familiar. We reach the corner of the street where we live. We see the A-shaped roof, the jewel box of my office, the face of my wooden giraffe in the window, the bruise on the peach that must be eaten in the bowl in the kitchen where now we stand. We unburden our bags and eat the last of the car chocolate and leave the kitchen and sit together in the love seat.

Time slides by.

An orchestrated triumph.

FOR AS LONG AS WE HAVE

We've never met, but I have read her, I have taught her, I am awed by her, I respect her, I am lucky, sitting here—she to my left and my husband to my right, the couple who invited her and me to speak at this conference sitting before us deciding on the mushrooms or the soup, another writer on the way. We could talk about the way she bent her genre. I could quote her lines and parse her structures and say, *And so I wondered: How did you do that?* I could say a lot of things, but she is speaking now. "Oh," she leans in close. "I'm in love with your husband."

And why not?

And look at him.

The bones of his face arranged like a well-made house. The freckles from a childhood of sun. The pure white hair, his illustrious hair. The way he was born for Levi's, waist 30. Years and so little vanity (no vanity) have stretched the leather of his belt, and the twists of leather that he wears on his right wrist are flecked with paint, and since he is wearing an actual shirt instead of the T-shirts that he favors, he has rolled its sleeves so casually and left the two top buttons open—another casual move; it drives women crazy. He wears his wedding-band gold on his right hand to protect the places on his left that were once damaged. "Beth, I think I might need to go to the hospital," he'd said, and when I looked, the sink was a pool of viscous red, and he refused to show pain because he never does, because he says I have enough to worry about, and because when you don't talk about something, it's less of a thing. His eyes are so dark they don't reflect me. His drawings are so strange that I've never been his model. He calls me Cuteness, and that is the only word I have to answer my own question: *How am I seen? How am I seen by him?*

"I'm in love with your husband." She leans. He's hardly spoken, perhaps identified himself with clay, or, more likely, I'm the one who identified, who boasted in on him upon introductions— described the glorious strange of his sketches, the antediluvian qualities of his clay, the buildings he drew, years ago, when he was the architect I married. I am responsible for this moment, I cut to this chase, I set this stage, I have acquired this annoying habit, for I know that the man I married charms, and that he charms precisely because he never tries to charm, and that, following a remarkable percentage of our social outings, someone will reach out across the ether and say, *I love your husband*—and so why not simply preempt the inevitable? The way he walks could kill you. The way he combs his hair with that right hand that wears the glint of gold. The way he doesn't realize what he's doing.

Can I get you anything? he'll say at night, when we are lying side by side on the family-room floor before a bad Netflix series or a good one, Rachel Maddow or Chris Hayes, the documentary he didn't think he'd like, but, in fact, he does. This is our ritual now, our best romance, something passersby would surely pass—these two middle-aged people taking in a show when it would be far more edifying or social or politically appropriate to be doing something more. He wants to know if he can get me anything, by which he means, *Would you like an ice-cream cone?* I'll feel him turn to look at me, to assess the obvious yes, to see whatever he sees in me, for I will never know. He will never write me, he will never draw me, he would never say; it is the secret that he will take to his grave, and may I never see that grave, may I be the first to go.

I'm in love with your husband, she said, they say. A year has gone by, and now it is late at night, as I write those words, as I lie, alone, in this bed, the windows open and the breeze coming in and the crickets sawing songs of love. Limb to limb, tree to tree, they sing. High or low in the unevenly cut grass, beneath weeds that might seem gorgeous. In another room, sleepless, too, Bill draws. A sheep with a man for a friend. Birds come to nest in the tufts of an old woman's hair. An angel suspended by strings. A girl lost on a familiar street. A jack-in-the-box blowing his lid. I am writing what I know and he is drawing what he imagines and the insects sing across the divide, and it all plays on, and it will until it doesn't, by which I mean (again), for as long as we have.

| daughter |

I am a daughter daughtering, in search of comfort, lost and abraded in the files of my heart. Please don't come, *my father says, and I obey him, or he says,* Please don't come, *and I come. Sometimes he worries I will talk too much or retrieve the old bone of our greatest contention. Sometimes he worries that I will scan his home—just two rooms now, where once there had been five and before that at least a dozen—and find something that will need picking up: the tie pin into the tie-pin box, the book to the library, the peanut-butter pretzels into the trash, for I bought them long ago. Sometimes I want just to sit and he wants just to move, and sometimes, again, we want the opposite.*

Do I reach across or keep our distance from the secrets that amass? Do I bring him gifts he does not want then watch as he preserves the succulents? Do I take him far, when near is safe, and is safe just more time passing? When daughtering is dutying, you hold nothing in your hands.

Daughtering cannot be dutying. Finish well, *my dear friend Ruta says.*

Sometimes I take my father to a river and we sit.

Sometimes I drive him to a garden and we wait.

Sometimes we don't talk and sometimes we do, not saying when, not saying how.

And every day, at eight a.m., he or I will call.

I am here.

Are you there?

Finish well.

CUT THE LIGHT

I drive the ribbon of road, past the black cows and the fishing stream, over the bridge, up the hill. My father steps across the threshold of the house he built for us, the house my mother burnished into home for us, the house we must relinquish now that my mother is gone. He slips inside my car. I drive farther west, forty-five minutes on country roads. "We're blowing this popsicle joint," I told my father on the phone, for there are crushed and wayward things on the opposite side of that door, there are stories that keep changing with each unloading and dispersal, there is everything we've found and remembered and put away or driven off to strangers, for without my mother here and with the clock ticking on, my father's moving. It's been months now, the two of us, finding and losing. "Wait for me outside," I said. "I'm driving."

We park. We walk. Toward the meadow. Past the Rose Garden. Down Flower Garden Drive. Past the lakes, the dragon-guarded tree house, and the beaded plumes of the Italian water garden until, in the near distance, we see the burnished heads of wild and seeding things. Stalks of yellow taller than we'll ever be. Blushes of purple and the wing tips of birds headed in and out of their boxy homes.

My father and I cross the bridge over Hourglass Lake. We stand and take in the unimpeded view—the distance between us and the farmhouse, the far-off fringe of trees, the tops of the hats of the people walking through. It's an Andrew Wyeth pastoral.

It is air that breathes.

Look at us, I think. We're breathing.

I stand with him. We walk. I predict the weather rolling in. Foresee the shortened days, the birds that will escape to warmer weather, my own self as I wake in the middle of the night and close the open window, a defense against the cold.

The meadow is bright. The meadow is crisp. The meadow wavers. We walk. On the ridge above the meadow, I find rows of white folding chairs. An anomaly, it seems. The chairs appear to grow straight out of the sandy soil, to be just another breed of grass and bloom. The chairs are a welcome strangeness, a temporary fantasia. Unpredicted. Unforeseen.

"We're rehearsing for 'Lost in the Meadow,' a site-specific theatre piece," a slate sign reads, and now I turn back around to study the meadow again, to try to imagine how theater gets done in eighty-six acres of birds and bees. I imagine sitting there and waiting for the actors to come—watching them rise up like mist from the plowed-down pathways with hawks on their shoulders and purple flowers in their hair.

I imagine what I cannot see—a daughter's job, a writer's privilege. I imagine the some day some time soon, when the house of my teenage years will belong to someones new. *It will happen, Dad.* Who they will be, how they will move, where they will rest their flowers, how they will sit in their own white chairs, at the edge of their own wilderness, waiting for the next act to come.

We walk on, my father and I. We wander up over a bridge, toward another tree house, to the edge of the forest, then turn back for the manicured grounds, the Peirce-du Pont House, the empty (for that moment) theater, the stone whispering bench.

We sit. My father at one end. Me on the other.

"Hello," I say to the stone. It carries the word across the long arc, to him.

"Hello," my father says back.

We sit far away, within a whisper's distance, waiting. We decide, in time, that we must return to the obligations waiting. To the boxes and the emptiness and the overriding question: Who will replace us?

And: How long before we'll be replaced?

It takes a long time, too long. It takes weeks and after that months, and, soon, seasons. I take photographs, I advertise, I write the pages you have been reading and place them in the local paper. We assure each other of our impending success. We avoid asking each other what is wrong with this house that my parents designed so that we might be happy, and then we ask, and then we remember that this is the house for which my father worked—weekends, nights, early mornings, always. This is the house that was always big enough, and always, thanks to my mother's gifts for hospitality and homemaking, *right*. Is it the hill the house is on that is the problem? Is it the curve in the road? Is it my mother's preference for green? Well, then, we'll paint away the green, and I will photograph again, and my father and I will protect each other from the rising bulk of disappointment. We will keep each other calm.

"It'll be fine."

"Yeah."

"It'll happen."

"Everything in its own—"

"Should we lower the price?"

"I guess. Maybe."

And then: A couple with a dog named George and a second child on the way feels, they say, the love and memories my parents' house was built of. They see, in the living room, their own Christmas tree. They imagine sitting in the glass room throughout a night of storms. They think—no—now they know, that they would like to buy it.

"Dad?"

"Beth?"

"Did we do it?"

"Maybe."

Before noon on a Saturday in June, I return to my father's house for the last time. The grass is growing between the driveway bricks. The spindles of new trees rise in the garden. I fumble with the key. I'm in.

It is wood and white, air and light, scatterings of gold, like kintsugi, in the hallway chandelier. The paintings are gone. The mirrors, the hooks, the holes, the flocked wallpaper, the carpet, the piano, the photographs on the piano, the orchids in the windows, the platters that stood on their sides to show their imbroglio of glazes off. No kitchen table, no sewing machine, no nineteenth-century portraits of Charles Dickens' niece, no carousel of slides, no chest of Kodachromes, no Maxwell Perkins first editions, no flying wooden pigs, no macrame tassels on hanging baskets, no tools, no ornaments, no four-foot-tall Santa Clauses. No beds to rest on. No chairs on which to sit. No books. No music. No one. Me.

I scour every surface, vacuum every floor, interrupt the spiders with their eyelash legs, remove the husks of two dead bees because I am so good at cleaning now. I stand in the fallen sun of the living room, where the Christmas tree once raised all its needle arms and the Regina played its music-box songs. I count the steps going up, measure the length of the hall, open the attic door to raw pine and stiff insulation. I stand at the threshold of my father's office and can see him there, in my mind's eye—work as his hobby, his consolation, his craft, the choice he made every time, still makes. I go back downstairs, into the master bedroom where my parents slept and my mother worked—a late-in-life college student. I circle again, I circle once more: into the dining room where we tried to be what we imagined families were; into the kitchen to open kitchen doors, kitchen drawers, the pantry, the cabinet where the bread would rise beneath a cool cloth. My mother's bowls: once there. The cranberry-colored glasses, the heat off the back of her pots, the crumbs beside her cookie jar: once and once and once and there.

Memory retains the smell of her tea. Memory retains parts and particles and I am thirteen, I am seventeen, I am twenty-three, I am a wife, I am a mother, I am angry, I have returned, I have loved her despite not always knowing if she loved me, despite suspecting that she favored others, despite being wrong sometimes and right sometimes, and there we are again, sitting (just us) at her table, before I understood that the end was near, when I thought—we both thought—that whatever had been ailing her had been, by doctors, cured.

We were celebrating cure.

I roasted you a chicken, Mom. I made the carrots like you taught me. See?

My mother died in this house. It had been a calamitous succession of illness and bad luck, worse timing, a stroke and then another stroke, after-the-fact heart surgery, coma, morphine. She had died and I had whispered to her, here, in this house, here is her essence, and now, leaving the kitchen, I make my way to the sunroom, her final room. I ease through the door, toward the window seat where the orchids were, where the sun reaches no soil. I sit, and it all comes back, her final days, the songs I sang to her, the recorder hymns my brother played, the hospice aide on the couch, the slow drip of the slow morphine, the hour I left when I knew she wanted the time, the space, to drift alone, when she had found, within herself, the impossible courage to pass on.

When I look up, I find a reflected me in the glass pane of the connecting door. I lift my camera and snap. *I will take you with me, Mom,* I think. *I will free you now from this room. Free us. I will never, until my dying breath, abandon you.*

I stand. I leave.

I climb the stairs again, now to lay out the scattering of boxes that my sister will, at last, take to her home. I begin the final check of closets and bathroom chests and built-in drawers, and the front door opens and my father has come. He stands a floor below me. Looking up. Weary.

"This house," he says, "has been an albatross around your neck. Fourteen months."

"I don't know," I say, because I don't anymore. "I'm sad for other reasons."

For suddenly, after all this time, after all this work and heartache, after all this hope, after all the months driving the neighborhood streets and stalking UNDER CONTRACT signs and texting the realtor and dying slow at three a.m., it is time, so soon, to go.

On a lazy Susan in the kitchen, I find two wooden dolls, side by side—a carved old man and lady.

On a hanger in my sister's room, I find my final skating dress, the competition dress—a square bib of pearls on a shiver of turquoise.

In the bathroom I find the yellow hair dryer that never fixed my curls, the towels we used, the towels we didn't.

In the kitchen closet I find a dusty cane.

In the garage I find more leaves to sweep.

On the top shelf in my father's office, I find an envelope of art, a yellow folder, the last photograph of my mother alive.

We cut the light.

Two hours pre-settlement, the realtor calls. She's at my father's house ahead of the buyers' walk through, and she has found one last thing, more evidence of my mother. Beneath the sink in the powder room there is, she says, a stockpile of tins.

"Tins?"

"You know. Tins. Like you'd use for cookies or sewing things."

"How many tins?"

"More than a dozen?"

"We swept that house like we were sweeping for explosives. And you found a dozen tins?"

"They're lovely. Really. I'll bring them to you."

A little while later, around a realtor's table, we are assembled — the realtor, my father, and me on one side, the buyers, their realtor, on the other. The title lady sits at one short end of the table. The banker guy on the other. Through the tinted glass we can see the fast gathering of clouds and the sudden white needles of rain. Inside one family yields a home, and the life of that home, and suddenly I am urgent with the need to pass on the house secrets, to lean across the table every time the banker or Sloane have stepped away to the machines and the phones down the hall. Orchids in the bay windows, I say. The roof tilts over the sun porch in the angle of sleep, I say. The bird feeders have been rigged so that the squirrels won't win, I say. We only sometimes used the laundry chute, well, really, we hardly used that laundry chute, but I mean: We did use it sometimes. We hid Halloween in the second attic.

I have a photo of my mother on my phone. I share it with the buyers. I have a photo of the orchids. That, too. I tell them how my mother is buried in a park beneath cathedral bells and how my father plants gardens by her stone and waters that garden and waits for the grass to rise, and how that is how my father has always been—taking such good care of us, of our house, of their house, soon. On the title page of a book I wrote I have scribbled down more stories—*We couldn't imagine all that our lives would become. We just knew that the house was a big and beautiful place, that the sun slanted in, that the birds came*—and now that book is in the buyers' hands and the banker's coming back, and more quickly now, running short on time, I name the rooms for the buyers. My brother's room. My sister's room. The room where my mother wrote her college papers.

"Dad," I say. "Dad. How old was Mom when she graduated from college?"

"Fifty-three," he says.

"Fifty-three," I repeat, as if this information is the source of every-thing, the soul center of the house that was built in 1973 and sold in the year 2016, and now the banker is waiting for me, and the title work is done, and my father asks me to remove the key from my ring and to give it to the buyers.

I give my key to the buyers.

We roll the chairs back. We check the tinted windows for the progress of the rain. We reach our hands across the table, and the buyers promise: *We will take care of the house. Our house. Yours.*

Back in my own living room, the realtor, my father, and I raise glasses of Martinelli's. We raise cookies, honey-mustard pretzels, cranberry Wensleydale cheese, tiny purple grapes. Slowly our eyes turn to the tins that Marie has expertly packed into a brown Rubbermaid. The tins are Nutcracker men. Funny houses. Peaches. Northern European Christmas scenes. Simplicity patterns. The tins, some of the tins, remain lined with my mother's aluminum foil, the creases where her cookies were, but the cookies are gone, but she is gone, but she kept these tins. She hid them in the powder room vanity that no one ever used.

"Mom's final gift," I'll tell my brother and sister later, when I divide them among us. Mom having the last word.

But the scene is reaching its end.

The scene ends.

"Beth," my father says.

"Dad," I say.

Our best words for each other.

LESSONS IN SOFT
AND HARD SOUNDS

I dream of San Miguel de Allende, I remember. Two thousand courtyards beyond two thousand doors. Sixty-four thousand feet above the sea. The whole thing coming into view off the long road from Guanajuato. Dry dust. Green knobs. Holm oak. Nopal cacti.

The Casa Quetzal, our hotel, seemed to have been carved out of fruit. It was bifurcated within—public zones, private ones, the corridors and terraces open to the sky. Bill and our son and I had reserved the rooms in the back, one stacked above the other and linked by a tightly helixed stair. We walked past the painted desk to get there, past the gardened breakfast cafe and the day's news, through a narrow hallway where bright red flowers sprouted from terra cotta pots against walls the color of picholine olives.

The farther we walked, the farther we were from the room we had reserved for my father, who was still new into the mourning of my mother, new into his life of just one in the house built for five, and just one in the bed built for two, and just one for breakfast in the morning, and just one answering the calls I made each day. *Hey, Dad. It's me. How are you?* The packing down and out of my father's big house was still a few years and tears away; we had not yet foreseen it. We only knew that my father was alone, and so we'd said, *Come with us to San Miguel,* and Bill's brother had come, too, and Bill's mother and aunt—two families merging in the midpoint aftermath of marriage between a Philadelphia girl and a Salvadoran son.

Bill was turning fifty. Our son, eighteen. "We'll have a party," we'd said. *I'd* said. But nothing was neutral in San Miguel. The place was full of opinions—the murmur of fountains behind padlocked doors, the inscription of grills high on windows, the casual flamboyance of the mariachi men, the coruscation, in the distance, of abandoned mining towns. Rose-colored spires pierced the sky. The smoke of elotes carts was weather. The lintels above the ornate doors were carved with the names of vanished families. And every day a boy wearing a cabled yellow sweater and shiny shoes carried a moose puppet across the cobbles of the town.

I didn't know where he was going.

I didn't know what he could want.

In a family of two languages, language might become a wall. For us, in San Miguel, there was the English, which everyone ostensibly spoke, and the Spanish, which worked particularly well for all members of the clan save for my father and myself. Our son had taken naturally to his second tongue. He spoke it, especially then, with what seemed to be grandmother-delighting ease. I spoke it not at all, though early in the marriage I had tried—Spanish books and Spanish tapes and eyes closed, lips practicing. I could not roll the Rs. I could not bear the necessary corrections of my timid pronunciation at the breakfast table, lessons in long and short vowels, soft and hard sounds.

But don't you want to get it right?

The Spanish of my husband's family sounds more like a party than English does, at least the way I hear it. It raises its voice, argues with itself, shivers and shatters and escalates and collides, and then everyone is laughing, the talk trills hysterical, the language cannot catch its breath. When we were all together in San Miguel, Spanish was spoken. Remembering was Spanish. Jokes were Spanish. Dinner orders were Spanish. Asides were Spanish. Architectural details were Spanish. Commentaries on the plaza, and the point is: I sat beside my father, at the table's edge. I stood beside him in the cathedral. I watched, with him, the mariachi band. I watched, with him, my son, who found all the words he needed, a distilled confidence.

Sometimes I'd pull my husband aside and whisper to him in our language. Sometimes, when I did, his mother would take his other hand and speak to him in Spanish. I whispered my English. She delivered her Spanish. His right hand, his left hand, until I sulked and my mother-in-law lifted her chin and my father—never a gossip, never a man who interferes, never a grandstander or a lesson-giver—boldly made no comment.

My marriage was alive and on display.

His marriage was something he remembered.

I was aware of this. I was embarrassed. Everything wasn't perfect because nothing is, and I was a little too good at the sulk.

It became easier to set out on my own with my camera—to be alone with the thoughts in my head, to find what I found to be beautiful and to frame that beauty without words. I photo-graphed the green cabs that drove through the streets between the in-leaning wedges of the walls. I photographed the cool in the wide cloister halls of the Escuela de Bellas Artes—the jungle of shade, bamboo, and fern, the orange trees and poinsettias, the working fountain with the Lamb of God, the room made twice its size by mirrors. I photographed the old couple choreographing a tango—he led, she followed; he stood, she flicked; he waited, she arrived; she put her foot down, so did he. They were together: two. They had survived their years. They danced the inverse of each other, which is to say they danced their difference in a room made huge by glass.

Out with my camera, I grew consumed with the idea of the photo-graphic edge, the counterpanes of juxtaposed things. The rough sweep of a hand across the gauze of a skirt. The blue against the green of the hills. The dark fingers of the boys releasing the white herons in a park. The tiny girl who hid behind the large woman selling bright dolls in the sun. The girl's smile. The doll-seller's scoff. The dry dust and the rain. The slippery shoes on the cobbled streets. The blazed afternoons and the cooled evenings. The birds that seemed to ring the bells in the church towers, the birds that, when the bell song sang, batted their wings to the far away as if the song they'd orchestrated were a kind of insult. And I kept flying away. And my father was watching, perhaps he was thinking, *Honor what you have, don't waste time being angry, everything ends, can't you see that?*

At night we closed the thick-hewn shutter of our one gigantic casa window, left our son in the first-floor darkness, and tripped up the helix stairs to bed. If it rained I listened to the hooves of the rain on the roof. If the sky was bright I imagined stars. When my husband slept I sorted blood and language, albondigas and bowls of coffee-flavored flan, the Philadelphia girl and the Salvadoran man. I sorted hierarchies—wife, daughter, self. I sorted the smile and the scoff. I thought of my father many rooms away, just one man in a room built for two, just one man in a bed, his first-born daughter butting up against the life she had chosen, beside the man she had chosen for the difference that he was—his fabulist Salvadoran self, his coffee-farm roots, his misted mysteries, his art, which is its own language, his languages, which are more than two.

The inconvenience of his complexity.

The art of the frame.

After rain, in San Miguel, the distant Sierra de Guanajuato range becomes a wild, soaked-through blue. The streets run with rivulets. The tin coffee cans fixed to the thick stucco walls glisten with pink and yellow flowers, and everywhere there is the spill of orange bougainvillea, there is the outrage of the beauty, there is the rough, there is the gauze, there are the undeflected angles, there are the edges, there are the overlaps of edges. There are the people who walk alone, and the people who walk together.

After rain, after breakfast, in the morning I would leave—head back out with my camera and photograph the stucco walls into which the broken parts of bells and wagon wheels had been shoved. I'd photograph the metal fence upon which old jeans had been slung. I'd photograph the peppers caught like fish by a hook, by a string. I'd photograph the pale cat touching a pink paw to the sky. I'd photograph the man who sold black hats. I'd photograph the steep hill I'd helped my father descend and the steep hill I'd ascended alone. I'd wait for the bells to ring in the rose-colored spires and the boys in the park to set the white herons free, and then I'd wait for the kid in the cabled yellow sweater to slide down the cobbles with the moose on his hand.

I don't know where he was going.

I should have known what he wanted.

My father watched, he waited, he never said a thing. Maybe he still hopes that I'll learn Spanish.

THIS BLUE JAUNT

My mother never traveled far, not after her legs were crushed beneath the wheels of a thief's getaway car. On good days she would drive her own lemon-colored Cadillac to the store or sit beside my father as he motored her to the Jersey Shore or endure the dozen hours of road to their summertime home on a South Carolina island. She could walk a block, or two, before things began to hurt. She could sit and watch the near whitecaps tickling the sand and imagine the shoals beyond her reach. She could suggest a city to which my father might drive, and, rarely, she would fly, but mostly she didn't have plane legs, or sea legs, or car legs, or legs that, after what we euphemistically called "her accident"—it was no accident—would heal.

When my father traveled otherwise, it was for business. Once to South Africa. Often to a small town called Oil City, where a subsidiary company that reported in to him had operations. Once or twice to Texas. But mostly my mother was my father's world, and when she died, his boundaries fractured.

He would have preferred a reason to stay home, but now there wasn't one. He accepted my brother's invitation to Peru. He accepted ours to San Miguel. He joined my sister in London and went up and down the Baltic Coast on a ship with strangers. He hadn't, in his newfound travels, seen Alaska. He wondered if Bill and I might come along.

"On a *cruise* ship?" Bill said.

"More like a NatGeo affair," I said.

When Bill sighs, it's like air being released from bellows.

A few months later we were off the ground, up in the air, looming over Sitka, "southeastern Alaska's only oceanfront town." Somewhere down there our next eight days lay—the *National Geographic Sea Lion* and its crew of underwater divers, kayak hustlers, anthropologists, and glacier hunters; the pantry with its overstock of meals; the passengers who, as it would turn out, bore intrinsically remarkable resumes. A famous *New York Times* columnist. The writer / consulting producer of a major TV show. An Israeli entomologist. A Canadian heart surgeon. Little blond cousins who wore matching blue pajamas and could belt the heck out of traveling songs. Two best-friend sisters approximately my age and an almost-teen who would read her stories to me and then listen as I'd read out loud, the lines of Anthony Doerr.

But we didn't know any of that as the prop plane landed and we didn't know it when we were transported to Russia-glazed Sitka, the hook-clawed birds of the local raptor center, the totem poles of an historical park. We didn't know what would happen when we boarded the *Sea Lion* the next day, our waterproof boots and pants and jackets consuming most of the room in our luggage. What I knew was that, upon a modest-sized boat among a healthy-sized crowd, I had arrived with two men, my husband and my father, who—most of the time in normal circumstances—are most comfortable alone. Bill in the basement with his clay or out in the converted garage with his drawings. My father with his spreadsheets and analyses, his long columns of repeated math.

After the raptor center and the historical park, after a first shared awkward meal, my father went out to the pier in Sitka, sat on a crate in his blue windbreaker, and looked out beyond the town, toward the strait where the brochure map promised we were going. In time other passengers joined him there, sat their luggage down, and waited, and some time after that the escorting began— the crew showing the passengers their *Sea Lion* rooms, the public and the private spaces. When the anchor went up, the boat shoved out. The white lighthouse with the red lid of a roof grew smaller in the distance.

My father watched Sitka disappear, and maybe, as he did, he thought of my mother and the friends she always had, the friends she would have made easily if she'd been on this boat, if she had the legs for that. I watched my father watching. I took his photograph. I would be, I thought, a bridge for him. I would help him toward friends while on a boat seeing Alaska.

It should be said that I love best the early-morning hours when my thoughts are my own. I love the scratched-glass bubble of a solo train ride. A solitary walk in search of turtle shells beside a lazy canal. This here and this now, this page, when memory is the other person in the room, the voice in my ear, the speculation.

Yet I have also become, even if I can't precisely narrate the gest, a friend. I have written about friendship. "Fluid, flexible, transient, unstable, supremely relative—friendship, the noun, is a juggler's term, perpetually changing hands," I declared, books ago, and in the years since, my friendships have changed—rooted in correspondence with the far-away, evidenced by the gifts that line my sills, suggested by the endless recharging of my phone, quantified by the warble of arriving emails and the ditty of fresh texts. My friendships are declared by the New Year's Eve tradition, the crabs I pluck from a friend's river, the tea I share in a florist's shop, the urgent hello hugs in a convention hall massed with thousands of book people.

I am known to listen, but within the brackets of true friendship, I talk. I have been accused of asking too many questions, of compounding conversation with elaborate extensions, and the accusation sticks. All of which is to say that Bill is short and to the point, except for when he's telling stories, and that my father is most at home in the consulting mode, grounding himself with other people's problems, and that I, when faced with the complications of society, do my utmost earnest best to shake myself from the province of my happy alone so that I might forge and friend.

There was the blue beyond of Alaska and the smoke of fog and clouds. There were the islands of terns and seals. There was the sea in the sky and the sky in the sea, and we were motoring on. "Fluke!" William, our Mexican whale watcher, would call. The passengers would gather in the cold mist—blankets around their shoulders, frost collecting on their nose tips—and watch for the humpbacks to crest, the mermaid-shaped tails to slice the air, then silently vanish. "White mountain goat on the hill to the right!" a guest would cry, and we would fumble with each other's binoculars. "Isn't that a puffin?" a child would say, and we would congratulate her for her expert eye.

When the *Sea Lion* stopped and anchored in, we'd kayak out to the shore and swish our not-entirely-waterproofed feet into the freezing water of the fjords and walk the difficulty-differentiated paths of the Tongass National Forest. We'd learn how to spot true Sitka spruce or how to blow a song out of long tubes of kelp or why we should not touch the starfish with the constellations on its back, the beating hearts of the jellyfish, the psychedelic crabs, the smooth gray stones with the white markings.

We'd hike desperate to see bears but hoping none would paw too close. We'd sing with the blond cousins or listen to the stories Ella would tell or walk in the shadow of the petite columnist— her red-plaid boots, her red jacket, her handsome profile—as she spoke of how to survive the loss of a long-loved spouse. We'd ask the TV writer for news of upcoming plots; he remained tight-lipped. We'd ask his brother, the entomologist, for news of bugs. I'd promise the two blond girls that I would name characters for them in future books (I did) and they would giggle at the promise. We'd settle in, mostly, with the best-friend sisters—arranging dinners with them, sharing snacks with them, heading out together in the kayaks with them, hoping that the humpbacked whales would not fluke beneath our rubber boats and holding, as we hoped, as we circled the broken glacier glass, the turquoise jewel-lets, each other's mittened hands.

"Dad," I'd say, bending toward him, "Tracey has a story you should hear."

"Kristi," I'd say, "ask my father about his days of mud in Fort McMurray."

"*New York Times* columnist," I'd say. "Please sit here."

In the short nights, Bill and I lay in single beds arranged in a tight-fitting, cabin-consuming L. We showered where the toilet was. We'd discuss Bill's need to be alone on a boat that was not built for solitude and how I myself was coping. I'd rise at three and walk the circumference of the deck, stopping for pods of killer whales, talking to William while the humpbacks fluked, sometimes joining the columnist on her morning constitutional. I'd photograph the blue upon blue, the white bounties of fog that ascended into clouds, the pink scissors of dawn. I'd think about my father, alone in a cabin of his own—my father, who had lost his long-loved spouse, who was packing up his long-lived life, who would be moving, soon, to the retirement village to make his way in the new world of what inevitably, as Abigail Thomas says, comes next. I would think about the day my mother died, and the calls my father made, and whether the sound afterward was the sound of silence or the sound that boundaries make when boundaries collapse. I would compare my husband's kind of alone in the English language to my father's kind of alone with his mind of math to my kind of alone which made room for many friends, and I would conjure me on that *Sea Lion* when the others were awake— hear echoes of myself at the dinner table or in the kayak or on the paths, seaming nearby people to nearby people, one moment to the next, my father to a friend.

We are here, I was offering, in my clumsy, conversation-extending ways. *Bill and I and the great elite of these temporary friends.*

Over the course of those eight days, the *Sea Lion* and its kayaks took us close to the glaciers so that we might hear the mournful cries they made as they sundered and crashed into the bitter strait. They took us by a stony shore where a big sleepy bear wearing a matted golden coat loped after ordinary seagulls. We were introduced to a native Tlingit interpreter and the legends of that place. We held melted ice-cream cones on Independence Day and watched the stars above reel like fireworks. We watched the brave among us plunge into the icy waterway and the crew wear Viking hats and the lonely anthropologist flirt with whomever he could flirt with. We were aware, each day, that one more day had passed, that we would soon be walking away from the jeweled sea, the blue, the temporary bridges I'd hoped to forge.

But I alone had not done the forging. I had, somehow, lost track of the friendships my father was making on his own, the plans he sealed without us. He'd take his own kayak, thank you very much, to the shore. He'd have someone (not me) strap him into his life vest. He'd take his own pictures and watch his own blue ice and on the last day at the breakfast on the *Sea Lion*, he had an announcement to make. I waited, and then, with a small flourish, he explained: He'd signed himself up for a float bush plane ride, a trip over a vast glacier on the *Pacific Wings*. He'd signed himself up with a friend.

But is it safe? I didn't say.

But are you sure? I didn't ask.

"With a friend?" I said, and he nodded. A smile on his face.

That very afternoon, as the *Sea Lion* anchored off Mitkof Island, my father flew. He went up and up and up, the pilot in the front and one of the sisters there beside him—the sister who, with him, without my help, without my unnecessary ministrations, had hatched the getaway plan. Alone, with her, he watched the melting glaciers glisten, he flew toward horizons, he disappeared into the blue. I watched him go from the shore, I watched him vanish. I stood beside my husband, my hands inside my pockets, where my hands belonged.

FAMILY RESEMBLANCE

At the retirement village where my father now lives, I am Mr. Kephart's daughter. He doesn't have to be anywhere near for others to proclaim it.

You must be—

You look just like—

Oh. What a startling resemblance—

My bones are his bones, my teeth are his teeth, my auburn tendencies are his. My anxiety, my guardedness, my discipline, my Ivy League choice, my outsiderly position—in these things I am my father's daughter, and because my father looks just like his father and because his father looked just like his, I am an exponential doppelgänger, an unoriginal.

We look alike. We are alike. We have respected, always, the other's sameness — assumed we knew the other well, assumed there was no need for questions.

Perhaps there are other identicals in my family tree, but my knowledge stops with my great-grandfather who, like my father, was named Horace. Horace Kephart the original is known still (by those who know him) as the Dean of American Campers, as a co-instigator of the Great Smoky Mountains National Park, as an author of books, as a small-town mayor, as the man who left his family behind to live the solitary. Ken Burns trained his documentary eye on him for *The National Parks: America's Best Idea*. Ron Rash flattened his character in his novel *Serena*. Charles Frazier acknowledged his scholarship on the last page of *Cold Mountain*. His eyes were two different colors, his life was academia and campfire, his dignity lives in the photographs, and he died on the road, in an apparent moonshine run.

Hearsay. Rumor. Spectacular contradictions. We chase the mysteries we can't solve, the ghosts we will not meet, the cajolery of the stories we must fabricate ourselves, the ironic icon. I spent years failing the original Horace Kephart in novels that didn't sell, in essays that didn't end, in bloviated blog posts. I spent years asking *those* questions. While all along there my father was, alive and present, a mirror to my mirror, thirty years plus two months minus two days implacably between us, now the auburn fading, now the strong bones bent, now the misbehaving teeth, now the silent stories seeping, now the vigil we kept during my mother's final months, the stone we designed for her grave, the sorting through and packing up of the house he built for us, the move into the village where I am, always will be, Mr. Kephart's daughter, and where the journey now is only sometimes forward moving, and where there are still thirty years plus two months minus two days between us.

And all the words we never said.

And all the questions I never asked.

And all the ways I lost by thinking that our similarities spoke for us. Of us. To each other.

My father and I walk the halls. We pass the nurses, the aides, the silver trays, the cloth wreaths on the ajar doors, the ungainly heights of the artificial roses, the motorized, the walkered, the enviably well-limbered.

Hello, Mr. Kephart—

You must be—

Past the blare of the TVs. Past the filing drawers of bubble-packed pills. Past Winston Churchill coming to us through closed captions. Out the door at last into the wide silence of a rooftop garden, where, in the shade we sit, my father and I. In his face is the age I will become. In my face is the age that he once was. In our family tree is the man who got away—the Horace who left the life he'd built for the life he wanted, who wrote of his escape this way:

To many a city man there comes a time when the great town wearies him. He hates its sights and smells and clangor. Every duty is a task and every caller is a bore. There come visions of green fields and far-rolling hills, of tall forests and cool, swift-flowing streams. He yearns for the thrill of the chase, for the keen-eyed silent stalking; or, rod in hand, he would seek that mysterious pool where the father of all trout lurks for his lure.

Now, out here in the shade, among the singe of the potted flowers in the molded soil, my father is the mystery. My father is the allure. My father is the truth I hope to find, give me time, give me more shade, give us the words we need so that we might say all the things we have somehow failed to say, so that we may set aside what we thought we knew, each about the other. My father is the story now that matters most to me: What he had wanted deeply, and how he bent time around him, and what it is to be him in this moment—the similarities only simulacrums, the past bigger than the present tilting toward no known, no certain future. Tell me, I want to say, what you might have been had you not been the father who chose to stay, the father who chose to give his children room to breathe and dream, the father who rarely intervened, the father who stepped back so that his one son and his two daughters could go whichever way they pleased.

You must be —

I am.

Sitting here in the shade in a rooftop garden, reading my father's face for the story that belongs to him and will, I hope, belong to me. Be earned, in time, by me.

BREAK DOWN

My back's on lockdown. I call for Bill and he rounds the corner—clay dust on his shirt, on his jeans. "What'd you do this time?" he asks.

"No idea. Sit? Stand?"

"Okay," he says.

The next day is worse. The third day is worse than the second.

Bill washes the clay from his hands. Grabs his keys. Pushes my lead feet into soft shoes and ties them. He drapes a jacket over my shoulders and helps me down the short hall, down the front stoop, into the Jeep—lifting my legs, my knees like they are some mechanical gadgets that do not belong to me. I wait thirty minutes for a doctor and three more minutes to be hardly seen—one hundred eighty dollars of inattention. I am sent home with muscle relaxants and painkillers, and I swallow them whole, struggle myself into submission, and wait. No miracle comes. Finally, some dry-mouthed sleep.

I open my eyes. It's Bill, that wedding band on that right finger of the wrong hand as it has been ever since that glass hummingbird feeder fell and shattered there, severing nerves and tendons. His hands, before that, had never been in question. He had, indefinitely it had seemed, perpetually escaped the threat, the civil war, the crash, the earthquake, the otherwise tragic. A man with a thousand lives. But now where the ring had been there is a swollen knuckle and a scar, and where there had never been a ring, there is one, and even in my haze on the chaise lounge, I notice the discordant ring and wish for eternal infallibility.

He hands me a bowl of applesauce. A spoon.

"Don't get up," he says.

I don't.

Over the next two weeks, medicine cancels everything. I am in a white, anesthetized place and nobody can touch me. I am responsible for not one thing.

You don't forestall a teaching semester. The day does come. There are four in an honors-thesis class—novels in progress told as victim, wink, equation, autobiography. There are fifteen enrolled in The Big YA—not memoir this time; I've been asked to stretch so I am stretching. Concept and conceit, character as story, symbol as narrative. Thirty-five texts, ten exercises, one final four-thousand-word project, and the first thing these fifteen will do is teach me what books are supposed to be.

What are we here for? I will ask them.

They will tell me.

First day Tuesday. The bag with the books on my shoulder is crushing. When the train pulls into Thirtieth Street, I take short, careful steps down the aisle and onto the platform where I again arrange the weight around my spine. My best imitation of decrepitude. I leave the station for the January streets of Philadelphia. I crooked-slice the Drexel campus toward Chestnut Street, crooked-slice the Penn campus toward Walnut. It's thirty minutes before my Honors meeting, and my phone is ringing.

My father has been ambulanced to the emergency room, my sister says. He is having difficulty breathing.

"Is he in danger?" I ask the nurse, once I reach her.

"Not immediate," she says.

I get a message through. Another message. *I will be there, Dad.*

But first: my four students on soft chairs in Kelly Writers House. But next: my fifteen students around one hard table in a Victorian manse. Halfway through Ursula Nordstrom, *Stuart Little*, and Markus Zusak, I am skipping pages, condensing thoughts, apologizing for the fumble. My father, I finally say, is in an ICU waiting. I have told him that I'm coming.

Go, the students say.

I zip into my coat, sweep my books into my bag, promise an extended evening email, then throw the weight of all I've carried onto my shoulder and tiptoe hurry the ten blocks to the train. From the train I jostle to the hospital. At the hospital I run to the elevator, then through the zigzag halls to the ICU, where I drop the bag at last onto the floor. We must wear masks to enter, yellow robes, plastic gloves. My father can barely see me. On the other side of his BiPAP breather I see him.

He talks into his mask. Long lost sentences. He accepts the nurses' pricks, the doctor's charts, the little white cup of pills, the 40 deviant mg of steroids that will deliver a massive shock to his executive function. Bill has arrived and gowned up, and we make no-problem talk. No problem, we're in the ICU. No problem, these machines, our masks. No problem, Dad, look at what good care you've got. You'll be fine. No problem.

There are days after this—the two of us in ICU lockdown, the two of us in sixth-floor step-down. At the end of the week, my father, alone, takes another ambulance ride to the skilled nursing center of his retirement complex, where he will stay for weeks as a man tethered to oxygen and treatments, a wheelchair, a walker, a man with sudden insulin needs, a man who calls me, shortly after his arrival, steroid terrified.

"Someone needs to crack the code," my father says. "We need an exit strategy."

"What code, Dad?"

"The virus code. Call your brother. Get him down here."

"What kind of virus?"

"A computer virus," he says. "The one that I am carrying. We're all in terrible trouble unless your brother cracks the code."

I gather family photographs and drive. I find my father in his new skilled-nursing room, the windows behind him yielding a view of his own villa where, only a week ago, everything was fine, was normal. I sit with him, knee-to-knee, forgoing the mask and the gown, the gloves, because there is only one thing that matters now and that is that he can hear me, that he beat the steroids, force of will, and remember who he is.

"Dad," I try to joke. "You're no computer virus."

I am not to be believed.

I lay an album across his lap—a book my brother once built out of the photos my father's father had taken. The first-page caption reads *Graduation Day, June 1952, University of Pennsylvania.* In the photograph my father's gown has a purple sheen. His collar is engineering yellow. His hair is auburn, his face is Hollywood, he's a Frank Sinatra kind of man, smart and kind and handsome.

"Look," I say, "at how beautiful you are."

He waves his hand, impatient, no time for this. There is viral wreckage coming. Massive meltdowns. Only my brother, my brilliant brother, can fix this thing, reach inside my father and crack this code, and look at all the time I'm wasting.

"You're not hurting anyone, Dad."

"I am."

"You've had a virus, a flu. You're getting better."

"Call your brother."

The next three photos are deeply shadowed—purples and blues. *Thanksgiving 1952. Luray, Virginia.* My father stands beside his father in the snow holding the broken spear of a stalactite in his arms. Next he stands with his mother at a Shenandoah overlook. In the third photo, it's my dad behind the camera, photographing his parents, and suddenly I realize that my grandparents stand at the same overlook where Bill and I stood, a few years ago, in the aftermath of a flood, with questions: What is next? How do we get there?

I turn the page. *Christmas 1952. Kep's Chevy.*

My father takes the book from my hands, lifts it closer to his eyes. Something eases. "Now that," he says, "was a car. Look at the whitewall tires."

"Fancy."

"Sold it when I joined the Army. Never had a car that nice since. Never got another car with whitewall tires."

He's not interested in *Summer 1955* or *Fall 1955*, or *September 1956*. He lingers over *Spring 1957, 19 Burns Road, Ashbourne Hills, Claymont, Delaware,* his first house bought with Army money. It's a plain split-level with brick base and a big bow window. The Chevy is parked in the unfinished drive, the grass is patchy, the front door opens to brand-new empty. "We thought the house was big," he says, "but it was small. We thought the backyard was even bigger, but it wasn't, was it? It was very small."

"It was a great first house, Dad."

He scratches his nose, doesn't think so.

On the pages now, my father and mother sit at the piano. My father and mother sit on the couch. My father and mother sit with a blond baby on their laps, my brother. Then there is me, in hooded pale pink. My mother holds me, my brother stands near, but it's my father in his spotted shirt and pinstriped coat who has all eyes on me.

"That's you," he says.

"Yes."

"And Jeff."

He turns the pages on his own now, skips ahead to *June 1963, 3023 Maple Shade Lane*, a house under construction. He is slender, still, standing back in the dried mud, a ladder stepping up to the unpainted shingles of the second floor.

"That was the house," he says.

"A perfect house."

"A real backyard."

"A creek across the street."

"A nice kitchen."

"That big room? Where we sang? Where we danced?"

"We were on our way, then, weren't we?"

"Everything we had, Dad, you gave to us."

He turns more pages, but he's getting tired, anxious again, derailed. He skips pictures of my mother, pictures of the house he loved, the house that would never be the same after our year in Boston, when the renters gave it all over to so many unannounced cats that every carpet would have to be torn out upon our return. He stops at an image of a gray floral couch against a blue floral wall. Jeff, his hair still light, reads to his sisters, two of us now.

"That's Janice," my father says.

"Yes."

"We were complete."

"We were."

"Beth, could you please call your brother?"

The nurses huddle, treatments wait. Blood-sugar pricks, pure oxygen, pills, a strong-armed occupational therapist who, after the briefest conversation, declares that my father is, like him, a problem solver. "We have a problem to solve, sir," this Michael says. "Number two is getting you back home. Number one is safety."

In between, I call Jeff. I explain, again, about the virus. "Can you confirm or deny," my father says into the phone, "that I am a virus?"

"I can deny," my brother says.

My father, despite being calmer, won't believe us.

"Dad," I say. "You are not a virus. You *had* a virus. You will not destroy the world."

"Jeff," he says. "You have to crack the code. They will kick me out if you don't."

We go through it again, my brother and I. The nurses return, I hang up, I let the experts in. I cede the hour and the day and the days to come to their expertise, their rhythms, their patience with the malicious steroids, which frighten my father from sleep and logic, though sometimes the steroids capitulate, and it is my father speaking, my actual unterrified father.

"Do you know what I did?" he says, one day. "Last night? When I couldn't sleep."

"I do not," I say.

"I calculated my last escape."

"Okay." I give him the eye. He gives me a long look back.

"I mean it," he says. "Listen."

He will break free from the bed and the tubes, he says. He will steal his own keys, steal back to his villa, pack nothing. He will back the Volvo out of the wide drive onto the easing curve and accelerate, all the way to Missoula. Montana, he says. Where no one will mind the older man at the deli counter—a sausage sandwich, please, mustard, a black-and-white milkshake.

"Crazy?" he asks, when he's done.

"Not crazy," I assure him.

"But then," he says, relieved that I am giving him this story, that I have not stopped him for a midcourse correction, "I realized: The police. Highway cameras. You would tell them that your father is missing. They would come searching. They'd find me. You'd be angry."

"No, Dad. I would not be angry. This is your life you're living."

"I wanted to go quietly," he says now, the dream dissipating. "I did not want this."

"You're going to be okay," I say. "I'm here. You're here. With me."

HERE IF YOU NEED ME

When they lose my father's medicines in the days and weeks, then months, to come, I demand emergency provisions. When it is clear that the wrong pills and the wrong doses have been slipped into the treatment, I am not easily consoled. When they accidentally bring my father someone else's cure, I am aggressively self-righteous. When the meals that are delivered aren't the meals my father wants, I knock to the front of farmers'-market lines so that I can hurry back to him with something he might like.

When there are bills to pay, I pay the bills; when there are calls to make, I make the calls, when the therapists and the aides and the nurses are kind, I bring them books, I bring them flowers, I bring them cookies; and when something goes wrong and then another thing goes wrong and when, now, no fault of his own, no forgiving this scenario, my father is newly quarantined, I declare, superhero style, *To hell with quarantine*. And show up. And do not don the quarantine gown, the quarantine gloves, the quarantine mask. And insist with my questions, until I get the news we must have, so that I can carry it back to my father, who lies in his bed and asks if, perhaps, I can just sit, if, perhaps, I can quiet now and be.

But this is his life I am defending.

This is his life, and I am turning:

Thin-lipped.

Grim-faced.

Narrow-eyed.

Drought complexioned.

When fighting on behalf of the father you love, who do you become?

Now it is decided that my father must move—from his spacious retirement village villa to a two-room fraction in Personal Care. Now I start the moving, winnowing, choosing, packing. I distribute and disseminate, negotiate the Steinway with the invisible cracked rib. I give my mother's vases to the aides I like most. I leave an oil painting of my mother young to curbside strangers then carry my father's future up the hill—lamp by lamp, suitcase by suitcase, salvaged plate by undispersed spoon, until the pressure is too big and I am far from big enough, and my brother arrives with a plan: We'll hijack a dolly to transport the heavier things. We'll get the heavier things transported. Then we'll nudge the empty dolly toward the downward curving hill, take a running start, and hop a ride, skateboard style, back to our father in the nearly empty villa.

It will be funny, trying to keep our balance.

It will be funny, if one of us falls off.

I wish I'd thought of that.

Proficiency is not benevolence. There is an art to being present.

In early May, I get into my car, pull up to the village, and park. I wave hello to the ladies who sit like brightly colored birds on the benches outside the Personal Care wing and walk the long hall where my father lives. Knock.

"Hey, Dad."

We head down the hall and slide into the sun. The ladies on the benches raise the wings of their arms inside their white and baby-blue cardigans. Their three-footed canes stand upright and steady—a miniature, silver, defoliated forest. Had I a bus I would sweep them up into the adventure I have planned.

I swap my car for my father's car and drive it nice, slow—giving him time with the handsome Volvo he has been separated from. I keep my hands on the wheel while he tunes his radio and adjusts the interior air, as he watches the forsythia in the yards we pass, so intrinsically beguiling.

I tell him we're headed to a garden. I tell him I'll drop him off at the entrance circle and then we'll walk not all that far and sit in the overlook for as long as he wishes.

I say it, I have planned it. Me. The daughter.

The rocking chairs are empty when we reach them. The garden hill decelerates at our feet. There is the green lean of particular blooming things, and we sit, doing nothing. If you'd look at us you might say we were perched on a low shelf of sky.

The clouds puff up like white balloons.

I take instruction from the hour.

When fighting on behalf of someone you love, the fight must end, the love must be the art of being present. I am slow to learn, but I am trying. Pastrami lunches. Riverbank afternoons. Conversations in the shade of village gardens. The art accelerates. I feel myself wanting more for him, more for us, more (the wanting hurts) for me. On a Saturday in July, I have a new plan, my best plan, I am certain. Bill and I will take my father to a hot-air-balloon festival. We'll watch inflated color take the sky.

Sure it's hot. Sure it's far. Sure it is no doctor's order. But look at us and look (this is me, wanting to see) at the love I give my father.

The crowds are thick when we arrive. The sun is cruel. The fence where we are to stand to observe the grand ascent might as well be on the far side of the moon. Bill heads off toward the clash of vendor booths and singers of songs, while I walker with my father over the ruts and provisional plank bridges of the festival grounds.

We stop for minutes at a time so that he can sit and rest in his collapsible chair. It takes us an hour, maybe, to get from the car to the fence, but we arrive, we settle in, I uncollapse his chair, I stand beside him. We are four or five hours from the main event and out there, beyond the fence, there is nothing but launch-pad emptiness.

They call the hot-air balloons the gentle giants. These envelopes and baskets lifted by fire and by air, directed by wind and cables. These touches of genius more than two hundred years old. Like everything that's beautiful, they're gored with danger, too, and I guess this is the part where I confess that the balloons are my obsession, not my father's, that it is me, not him, who has spent four years writing a novel about them, lusting (that is the word) after hot airs.

I tell my father some of the history I've read, some balloonery stunts and heroes. I tell him what I hope we'll see. I stand and he sits and we are side by side, squinting toward nothing, and Bill is wherever he is. He texts me sometimes, speaks of shade and a cool Pepsi.

When my father asks for water, I am glad to run and get it.

When my father remembers that he left his afternoon pills in the car, I run again, return.

When I run out of balloon exempla, I have nothing more to say.

The excoriating weight of the sun.

The excoriating waiting.

Three o'clock.

Four o'clock.

Five o'clock, and back at my father's retirement village, dinner is being served in a well air-conditioned room on clean white plates with proper silverware. Five o'clock, and the ladies on the benches might have sung today, might have even sung Sinatra, may be eating sugar-free ice cream in sugar-free cones waiting for the movie to start in the comfortable villa auditorium.

"Sorry, Dad," I say.

He waves his hand, brushes away my apology. His hand, I fear, is burning.

Six o'clock, and Bill emerges from his tunnel of shade and finds us. The crowd behind us is wide, wild, festive—lounging on blow-up chaises, standing beneath big-lid brims, wearing rainbow-colored glasses. Six o'clock, and in the distance, a human cannonball is about to be shot straight from his cannon, and the crowd stands, it binoculars up, and we have no binoculars.

"Can you see him?" my father asks, for he's standing, too, leaning all his weight onto his walker in the rutted earth.

"That way." I point, and my father leans harder and squints more but cannot see him.

The cannon blasts. The man flies. He is saved by the nets strung up to save him.

"How'd it go?" my father asks, over the roar of the crowd.

"Well," I say, and my father shrugs.

Now, when we return our gaze to the main attraction, the launch field is being recast as a theater. The ballooners are arriving with their Avis trucks, their pickup trucks, their stars-and-stripes-painted trailers. Entire crews pile out of vehicles, clown-car style. Children run up and down the field. Tarps are snapped out, bundled balloons are unbundled, baskets are given a little shine. The fancy people who will be sent aloft are gloriously fancy, while the regular sky riders fix their caps. The empty field is now a psychedelic one. A fan turns on, a single fan, and the first balloon inflates. It lies on its side stretching its long stripes out.

We have front-row seats. We avert our eyes from the sun on the horizon. We wait.

"Do you want to sit?" I ask my father, but he can't hear me. He's lost the batteries, he pantomimes, on his hearing aids. He will watch the spectacle of hot-air balloons like a movie with no sound. He will watch it standing.

The first balloon inflates. It bobbles. It lifts itself from its supine state and becomes a proper, upright teardrop. It tugs at its cables and the ground crew tugs back, and now into the basket its pilot climbs. I can hear the propane burner burn. My father can see the blasts of fiery breath. The ground crew gathers for one last touch of the basket, one last conference with the pilot, and then the cables are released, and the burns burn, and the balloon lifts, and something in me swells.

My father stands.

He leans across the fence.

My father is amazed.

The breathing lungs of the once-dormant balloons. The peaceable chaos of stars and moons, greens and yellows, weaves of primary hues, rip locks, parachute tops, insignia and brands, a panda. We never know, when a balloon begins taking its airy shape, what it will turn out to be, or how it will soar. Stripes and diagonal splits, an American flag, a blue dog, that panda, and the crowd is thick with joy, the crowd sings to the songs that the loudspeaker blares, the crowd is one single thing on the ground and the balloons are their singular things in the sky, all streaming breezeward in the same direction, over our heads, away from the sun, to a not-so-distant touchdown, and now even the official photographers have stopped taking photographs to watch. When one balloon nudges another during takeoff, it is not a nudge, it is a kiss, and we roar.

I touch my father's shoulder so that he can watch my lips.

I touch his shoulder so that he will turn, so that I can see his face.

I touch his shoulder and the balloons are in their floats—their fires hissing, the pilot hands waving, the music playing, the breeze behaving, and up they go, up higher and breezeward, like musical notes, like a harmony sung only in soprano.

I feel the heat of a tear in my eye. I feel myself exhaling, and *beautiful* is the only word I have, beautiful, and my father has seen this, he is standing right here, he is at the fence looking up.

Nothing tethered. Everything released.

We stay until the very end. We stay until Elvis himself, in fabulous shades and a durable belt, wobbles up, stories tall, and cants and tilts then lifts then drifts into the sky, follows the waft, the glide, the effervesce. We leave only then, and it is almost nearly dark, and there are ruts and planks and wobbles and crowds between where we are and where we must be and only so much time if we are to take my father out for the meal we promised him.

Bill goes off with the heavy things. I stay behind with my father. For every step he takes, he must first find solid walker ground. For every step ahead, there is a step or two to the side. The entrance gate is now the far side of the moon, and the crowd rushes past, and Bill is far ahead, and the night comes on us fast.

"Dad," I keep shouting, so that maybe he can hear me. "It's okay, Dad. You've got this," because what other choice does he have, what other choice have I left him with? *You've got this, you've got this, you have come this far,* but he is exhausted, his legs are folding, he is pitching back—leaning away from his walker and now all 107 pounds of me must be his bulwark, his defense against a fall, and I am not big enough, I am not big enough for this thing I made out of the love I keep transmuting.

The balloons are long gone, the effervesce. It is my panic, rising.

"I need some help!" I begin to call. "Help! Help *me!*" Until Bill, far ahead, somehow now hears me. He circles back. Catches my eye. Sees the sharp anxiety. Calm, he talks to my father, then walks ahead, marking out the best, least bumpy path, showing my father how it gets done, showing me. We go sideways, backward, forward. We arrive, at last, at the fairway and the vendor booths, and it's not that much farther now, I think, you can do this, Dad, I think, but he stops. Just stops. Begins that awful pitching backward thing, like a tree going lateral. There is a crowd behind us, pressure. I turn to apologize for the obstacle we have become.

"No, ma'am," one man says to me, a sturdy man, the closest one. "Don't you be apologizing, ma'am. We're here if you need us. We've got his back."

Here if you need us. The art of being present. My eyes grow hot with gratitude, while, over there, Bill finds Security, Security calls Medical, a lady at a booth lends us her hand. We uncollapse my father's chair and he sits with his collapsing legs and we wait until the medical people in their golf-cart truck come, their flashing sirens on. It takes many of them to lift the one of him, and Bill runs toward the car.

"Hold on," the girl in the makeshift medical transport says.

"Hold on," and she's talking to me.

The hour is dark. The moon is full. The moon is nearer than it's been. In the back of his Volvo, my father watches the roads, the world now asleep, all the restaurants closed. He cannot hear for now, and so we do not speak.

Here if you need us, the man said. *Here if you need us.* Such a simple thing.

It is so late at the villa that they've locked every door but one. The cafeteria is dark, the halls are empty, the ladies who like to sing are sleeping. It is so late, and it is so bad with my father that a wheelchair is now needed. Bill parks and I dash inside. I find what I need in a closet of emergency provisions. I wheel my father down the many halls, unlock his door, push him in. The only food in his place is a tub of sugarless cookies. He clings to his last bottle of water, his empty yellow bag of pills.

"That'll do," he says, when we're in. "I'll take it from here."

"Dad," I say. "I'm sorry, Dad," and give his burnt cheek a kiss.

The next day, early, my father calls. The next day his hearing aid batteries are working. I answer the phone with an apology, an apology that I have prepared during the night of my not sleeping.

"No," he interrupts. "It was beautiful. It was really something to see."

"But, Dad," I say. "Your legs, Dad. The heat. I shouldn't have . . . I thought maybe . . . I don't know what I was thinking."

"I don't know how they do it," he says. "Do you? I don't know how the balloons don't get in each other's way, but I'm glad I went."

There's silence, then. No questions and no answers and no good words to say. Love is not strategic. Love shouldn't be.

"Maybe you can send me pictures," my father says then. "So I can show all my friends over here."

"Pictures?" I say.

"Yes. A lot of pictures. Wait until they see."

PANIC ATTACK

The mice are running through the walls. They're drunk on speed, they're acrobats, they've got a Ferris wheel going and a carousel, a trampoline, a rock wall; they're playing Ninja Olympics and every one of them has won. They're wrapping medals around their necks, and the medals thud against their furry chests, and they thud and they thud; there are victory laps.

Just sleep, Bill says.

Who sleeps?

My father fell. He hit his head. I wasn't there. Two ambulances came for the one of him and the bump on his skull, no bruise. When I got to the hospital the next morning my father's voice was hoarse, the kind of hoarse you get from screaming. *Spinning*, is the word he said.

spinningspinningspinning

There were ninja mice in the orbits of his head.

He didn't say mice; he said fish. He said there were two fish on the wall, one red and one green, and that the fish were swimming, could I see them? He said he fell inside in his bedroom, but he fell outside, on the cement—his hand reaching for the arm of a bench, his new cane flying. He said he'd walked too far and gotten lost, that there was a hill, and that he'd gone wobbly-legged as a drunk up that hill, and on this point, though I have never seen my father remotely drunk, I did believe him, even if he would not look at me when he talked, or when he screamed, hoarse, *spinning*.

There is security camera proof of where and how my father fell. The evidence shows that there was no daughter beside him.

The doctors came in and out of the hospital room, the therapists, the nurses. When they moved my father, turned him, twice CAT-scanned him, sat him up for breakfast, checked his heart obsessively though his heart was not at fault, he was spinning. The world was above him like a squishy balloon, and he was on the bottom of it, flattening.

Dad, I said. *I'm here.*

I wasn't sure if he could see me through the spin.

The September hospital room was not like the January hospital rooms; it was so much bigger and its windows that much cleaner. There was a perfect view of the many gray days that we'd had and would be having, and I wasn't there when my father fell because two days before, sitting in the retirement village garden, he had said that it was time that I come to see him less, that I had done enough, too much. I had brought him flowers, and they were pretty flowers, and I had taken him out for his own banking, his own Staples shopping, his preferred restaurants, his camera store, to a rocking chair in a public garden, but now he was telling me that he wanted time alone, time to harbor and protect his secrets, a definition of *fair*, he said, that wouldn't be my definition of *fair*, and it was his choice, he said, to make — which fair was fair is fair — and so I should let him be.

He said.

And maybe my face was hard, maybe I was marionette grim, middle-child ugly, inflexible with my forgiveness in that moment on that point, and maybe on the way home I pounded my fist and maybe at home to my husband I cried, saying some things about what and which fair, too many episodes of the no-Merriam-Webster's *fair*, for this, in fact, is what's really fair, and how, after everything, all I'd wanted was time with my father. Transparent time. Unwithholding time. Honest time. But *Go*, my father had said — and that was a Thursday afternoon and on a Saturday he fell, and his world, he said, was spinning. The orbits and the orbitals were spinning.

A small bleeding on the brain is what the doctors said.

Dad, I'm here, is what I said.

Beth, you're never here, is what Bill said.

"Make no mistake," the anthropologist Loren Eiseley once said. "Everything in the mind is in rat's country. It doesn't die."

The mice are the ninja circus come to town. The mice have brought the elephants with them, the lions and the clowns, the miniature Olympians. When I close my eyes in the dark I see their steam-punk operation—the pipes and struts and two-by-fours from which they swing and swirl.

Sometimes the mice are behind the mirror wall and sometimes in the bathroom and sometimes I hear them in the kitchen downstairs, swishing and giggling, bellies bloated, bellies up, bellies digesting my granola-bar nuts, and if my heart would stop thudding I would not see the mice, I would not worry the mice, I would loosen my anxious grip on the mice and on my own anxiety, and I would sleep so that tomorrow, and the next day, I would be the calm, good daughter that my father needs, the kind of daughter who might, with pleasantness of aura, ease my father into believing that he will not fall again. I would be the calm, good daughter who banishes every anxious thing.

The doctors are depending on me. The therapists and the nurses. My brother, my sister, my father, too.

Diffuse the anxiety. Help my father breathe. Forgive.

You will not fall again.

The world won't spin.

The fish will swim away, and they'll keep swimming.

But the mind is rat's country. If you fall once you could fall again. If the world spins it could never stop spinning. If the fish break free they could keep breaking, and what is fair is never fair and it won't be, and I am spinning.

Dad, I say. *I'm here.*

~❦

I need to tell you something. I need to make this true. There is a cost to the cost of vigilance. There is something else, something more that happened when my father said I was to stay away, that his secrets held more value than my company.

It's this: Before that Thursday, two days ahead of the fall, I had been a daughter who ran to answer the phone. I had jabbed a finger. I had said hello. I had listened to find out. Was there a problem? A concern? I had been a daughter sturdy in her attention, dropping the present moment for the ringing phone. Dropping everything for her father.

But on the Saturday two days after that Thursday I had spent with my father in the retirement village garden, the phone rang and I didn't answer. The phone was sitting right there, on the couch beside me, and I was reading, also breathing, and I did not answer. It can wait, I thought. It can wait. *We* can.

The rare self-assertion of the grim-faced middle-aged daughter.

One hour later my sister texted: *I don't think it's a big deal, but Dad fell and hit his head and is in the hospital.* All that evening long, I was on the phone with nurses and a doctor, with my father himself, and the next day, during a storm, I drove to my father's apartment to get the things he would need for this hospital stay—a hospital too far away. At the retirement village I spoke with nurses, searched for witnesses, asked the question: *How did my father fall?* As if I did not know how he had fallen—he fell without his oldest daughter. Then, his hearing aids in hand, his batteries, his books, his socks, I got lost driving on roads mostly closed for repair. I got lost in the storm. Reaching the hospital at sodden last, I ran up the stairs and tripped and almost hit my own head.

Like father, like daughter to the end.

You can't turn away, even when you're asked to turn away. You can't turn away, even when you agree to turn away. You can't. You do.

"They are merely carried, these disparate memories, back and forth in the desert of a billion neurons, set down, picked up, and dropped again by mental pack rats," wrote Eiseley. "Nothing perishes, it is merely lost till a surgeon's electrode starts the music of an old player piano whose scrolls are dust. Or you yourself do it, tossing in the restless nights, or even in the day on a strange street when a hurdy-gurdy plays. Nothing is lost, but it can never be again as it was."

An anxiety attack is a direct response to an obvious but transient potential crisis. A panic attack is a shot out of nowhere dark, and it might not go away, it might just stick around and kill you. I'm good at both, of course: I am my father's daughter.

A brief history of my personal outstandingness at panic and anxiety:

I'd given a talk and people came. I'd given a talk well and the line was long—strangers buying books, an unusual Beth thing. All day long I'd been at this hosting university. All evening long I had read and answered and signed and it was almost nine at night, and they were turning out the lights, and there was just one more person wanting the inked-in letters of my name.

She had a question for me: *Why?*

Why what? I asked, with all my pleasantness, her book in my hand, her pen.

Why would you write a book like this? she said.

I looked up now. The pen was spotty. *Why wouldn't I?*

I don't know, she said. *It just seems like you'd not write this book—like you'd write another one.*

I worked to maintain my pleasantness. I shrugged. I signed. I went home. I changed. I went to bed. I woke in terror at two a.m. for someone had pinned me to the bed. An iron stake through my heart, my left arm thudding.

Bill? I said.

Bill?

Mmmm? he said.

I am dying, I said. *I'm already dead.*

You should try to sleep, he said.

But it was too late, the damage was done, the words of the stranger were in the blood of me, they were the platelets, the full-on physiology. *It just seems,* she'd said. *Fraud,* she might have said. *You are no writer.* For wasn't that the nature of her accounting?

Wasn't that the point, the message she had been sent to send—
to inject into my bloodstream, to infect me. *Why?* Indeed. Why?

And so the attacks began. Panic was my new best friend. She
was petite and curly headed. Wily and well-heeled. She carried a
hammer and an iron spike. She waited at my side. She attacked me
from behind. She was endurance, the ultimate marathoner.

Shaking me in the dark and rushing me down the stairs and putting
me out on the stoop beneath a cold, blue moon, still sweating.

You are not who you wish to be, she would whisper, arranging her
curls.

Your husband does not love you.

You don't deserve your husband's love.

*Your son is such a beautiful son and you could have done more, should
have done more, could have been a better mother, his life could have been
better, and by the way, your age is showing, your age is advancing, your
age shall henceforth be so unrelenting, and you made wrong choices,
you wrote wrong books, you cannot resurrect the past to fix it. Your best
friend is me, and I am panic.*

I went an entire month, once, without sleep, thanks to my panic.
You say it can't be done; I say I lived it. I say that I downed pink
pills and red wine, but nothing doing. I say I watched bad TV at
three a.m. Still, the sleep-negating panic. I say that I stood in the
biggest room of this small house, before the biggest window, and
watched for fox or, I don't know, owl, in desperation for another,
more appeasing companion, but I was adrenaline sick on panic;

she was all over me, all inside of me, all empowered with her heels, her hammer, her rusting iron spike. I say I was pale and weak and sometimes angry, sometimes making noise to wake my husband, because what is fair is fair after all, and why should I be the only one about to die of panic? Why should my troubles not be his, compounded? There is a marriage contract.

In the end, I slayed that marathoning panic. In the end, I fell asleep at last, gripping one notebook and a single willing pen. The pen was bleeding. It had written:

You said, What is the color of the shadow
On the snow? pointing to a place
Beyond our reach; I didn't know.
The hour was changing the color anyway,
And a tree was moaning with the cold,
Threatening misery. I tried
To kiss you, but you turned
Just then and stood yourself
Tall and were not mine
To claim, and besides, you know
How the wind can howl
In winter and the seeds down deep
Won't speak. That night
The moon was going to be full,
And the snow was going to be lavender,
And we would sleep alone,
Or perhaps you slept,
While I waited downstairs for a poem.

I wrote and, in writing, I bored panic so thoroughly with the intimate instant that she turned, and I closed my eyes, and she was gone, but gone just temporarily.

There would, of course, be more. The transient potential and the nowhere dark. The thing with the curly hair and the Lady Gaga heels and the shame that comes when the radio host asks you a question, live, and you can't remember (you are sudden-anxiety-onset paralyzed) how to answer, and the awfulness when you don't recall (sudden onset) whether the red light or the green light is the stop light or the go light, and the danger (sudden onset) of your blood thudding so loud about your ears that you cannot hear whether the man is saying if it is time to put the fire out. Or stupid things, like the thirty times each day your heart knocks fast because you're sure you have lost the necklace you've been wearing, are still wearing. Or the several times each day you check for your wallet, even though you have not left the house, even though you haven't moved your wallet.

Otherwise, though, you're fine.

Why, indeed.

After the hospital, after the bleeding on the brain was past, after vertigo had been ruled out but the doctors still had not tamed the spinning, after it was clear that a form of restlessness and agitation, a slurring of language and logic had set in, a condition I had no name for then, a condition I would only later read about—ICU delirium (hallucinations, muddled thought, muddled language, anxiety, depression)—after it was clear that treating this derangement was not part and parcel of any official plan, my father was returned not to his two nonspacious rooms but to the rehab wing of the retirement village.

Here there would be trays brought to his bed, medicine ushered in on wheels, nurses on either side to help him up and through, physical therapists and occupational therapists to measure his blood pressure when he was sitting and standing, to walk with him carefully when he was walking. There would be this, and there would be me, doing my non-onset best to topple the strangers who were living in his head.

Cursor, lock and key, computer program, keyboard, my father said, meaning, I would learn: *I need to go to the bathroom.*

That thing, with the you know, he said, and so I would stand there, guessing, laying out simple words like a smorgasbord from which he might pick and choose his desperate meaning.

Just have fun with him, a doctor said, but I said, *The current situation seems to call for something more.*

Your father will make all the decisions here, the nurse said. And I said, or wanted to say or tried to say, *But first we have to get my father back.*

He thinks we're stealing things, another nurse said. *He doesn't think that*, I said. *That's not him speaking.*

Make it incremental, take it step by step. Declare the fish mere figments, for they are. Substitute right syllables for wrong syllables and make him repeat after you. Show your father the wallet, then have him show you the wallet, until the wallet is right where it belongs.

What we do.

What we did.

Father. Daughter.

And pay the bills, and talk to lawyers, and bring him books, and remove the books, and not flinch when he announces a sudden distaste for F. Scott Fitzgerald. Take him out for air in a wheelchair ride and park him near the aide singing Nat King Cole to her sleeping charge and get him all tangled up in a conversation about old-days Atlantic City and nudge his wheelchair toward the sun, for how he loves the sun; he sleeps there. Then roll him back to his rooms again—the rehab room, the two nonspacious rooms—and say again the words he needs, which are not *cursor*, which are not *lock*, which are not *key*.

My voice growing hoarse with the insisting.

You are fine, I kept reminding him. *Fine*. You are lucky, even: no broken hips, no broken skull, no continuous brain bleed. And some hours were good and some hours weren't good and sometimes, after I got home, he would call me, panicked:

Where is my wallet?

Right where we left it.

Trust yourself, Dad, I kept saying.

Beth, where is my wallet?

I try to avoid the things that make me panic. I try to dispel the rush. I try to confound the curly-headed intruder, avoiding all known triggers. This includes choosing stone-cold silence over direct confrontation. This includes maximum-security budgets, so that I won't risk overdrawing my account or jeopardizing small but worked-for nest eggs. This includes packing the minimal least when I leave the house—less to be lost, less to be patted down excessively, less to be preemptively mourned (but what if I *had* lost it). This includes not flying on planes when I don't absolutely have to and not standing around fires that must be extinguished and not looking in the mirror in the morning and, for god's sake, not looking at the goddamned photographs. This includes avoiding the things people write about me and not asking others why I don't matter enough to be written about. This also but of course includes no longer hanging myself on the ropes of radio or TV.

I am bigger than you, panic.

I am ready for you, panic.

I will not capitalize you, panic.

You cannot break me.

She breaks me.

The other night when I woke to the sound of the mice gone to scamper in the wilds of the walls, I was 100 percent absolute that masked criminals had broken in. Every ricocheting swoop and shuffle was, quite obviously, the echo of a murderer headed straight for me. Every carousel turn was an underworld creature set heinously free to roam and ravage and ruin me.

I'd left my phone downstairs.

My husband was fast asleep.

My heart was a big black bird slapping its wings and at the center of the bird was the spike that panic brings.

Bill, I finally said. *Do you hear that Bill?*

Must be mice, he said, when he heard it.

Mice?

Mice. You could hear them squee.

It was time. It became time to move my father. To carry all his things from the rehab unit in the village to the two nonspacious rooms in the less-than-independent wing. To replace, to rearrange, to welcome him back to what we had not yet called home. I was in charge. I had a system. I put on my tiptoe self and talked my father through every broken-into-tidbits moment.

Now I am packing up your socks. Now I am packing up your pants. Now I am packing up your books. Now here's your wallet. I'm going upstairs and then I'll be back down, and yes, I have talked to your nurses, I have talked to your friends, I have told everybody that you are, yes, coming — what was the word? Not *home*.

He had told the nurses that he wasn't ready, but he was. He had told me not to come and then he'd called me back and told me to come early, and I didn't let the phone merely ring-a-ling this time. I was vigilant. I was on it. I was the good and calming non-onset daughter.

You're going to be fine, Dad, I said, but I could see the wings of the big black bird through the walls of his chest, I could see the whites of anxiety in his eyes. I could hear the draw of his breath in his anxious lungs. I could hear the scramble of the words in his head — words going around in a carousel tumble — and I could see what I had to do: not be the one who panicked.

I did not panic.

One minute by one hour by one morning by one afternoon by one night by one day by another.

He settled.

He did it.

He beat it.

Take that, ICU delirium. Take that, sudden-onset.

If I open the door, the air comes in. The air is green, and it is blue. It carries the sound of the howl of the child next door and now the child's mother, talking casually with another. The boy's howl, apparently, is not a howl worthy of attention and it will fade into itself and be forgotten. It will be a lesson to the child: prioritize your fear, calm your rage; you are responsible for your own panic.

A bird now, out there in the air. A car on its take of asphalt. If I think the word *grace*, my head will hurt less, my pulse will unquicken; it will be like I am writing a poem. So I think the word *grace*, and now it might be a toad out there in the air or a self-satisfied insect or the soft paw steps of the neighborhood deer—no, owl—no, fox. It might be anything on tender toes. It might be friend, not foe.

How are you doing? my father called today and asked me. He is good today. He is more than good. He has a whole week planned out, and he has planned it well: a movie, a concert, a recital, a lecture—all happening right there, in the village that does not, at this moment, need a daughter.

I'm a little tired, I said.

Tired? he said. *Why is that?*

I told him about the mice and their Ninja Olympics. I told him about the sound of the medals around their necks. I told him I thought a stranger had broken in. That someone was coming for me. Something.

Oh my, he said. *Oh my. What will you do?*

The things one does, I said. *I guess.* Though it pained me to think of stopping any ninja short. It pained me to be the cause of another mouse's panic. It pained me to think of killing a mouse, when all I actually wanted to kill was my panic.

Beth, my father said. *You need to do this right. Call in the pest people. Will you?*

I'm good, Dad, I said. *I'm good. I promise,* but he wanted none of that.

No, he said, *you have to do this right. You have to let me help you.*

THE WEIGHT OF
MY CONFESSIONS

Then the mice moved into the engine of my father's car. They warmed their little tummies there during an icy stretch of winter. My father had loved to drive; he had loved his cars. We'd clung to his silver Volvo with the thin red stripe long after he himself could sit behind the wheel so that I might, a few days a week, drive him in it. To lunch, to the bank, to Staples. Best: down roads we hadn't driven before, beneath shade that felt tremendous. "We're going to blow your popsicle joint," I'd say, and then I'd drive the miles to his retirement village in my volcanic orange Mini, park, climb into his sterling Volvo, and chug to the curb where he'd be waiting.

The car was a relic from before, a small museum of memories from his adventures on the road. It smelled, to him, of speed and dare and luxuriated afternoons and the freedom he had had to go wherever the roads could take him. It wasn't some institution with whisking doors and café hours and name tags on the doors, that car. It was, instead, his mobile dream, his sweet esprit de corps.

I'd toss the walker in the back, I'd nod my chin. I'd fit my hands to his steering wheel, and we'd be off. He'd fiddle with the temperature. He'd lean to gauge the gas. He'd turn the radio symphony off or on, and at stop signs he'd tell me when it was my turn to go, at red lights he'd tell me to keep edging right, when the road divided into two lanes, he'd tell me which lane to choose, how fast to go, when to brake.

But during that one icy winter stretch, two friends had lost their young children—one to suicide and one to cancer. The memorial services were all day and one was at some distance. The long talks on the phone had left me broken—what can be said, of suicide? what possible help is consolation? For that crushing interlude I did not drive the half hour to my father. I worried, in my own house, about the Volvo sitting there, stuck-still. I mentioned my concern over the phone. I hoped my sister, staying at the retirement-village hotel while visiting her daughter, might rev the engines to keep the machine working-order well, but it was so cold outside, and, besides, my father said, I'd get back to it all soon enough.

Winter.

One week later, when I turned the ignition key in my father's Volvo on the coldest day of all, something thumped and spun, something stalled. I'd brought Bill along, for I'd feared I'd need a cool, mechanical mind to overcome the three-week no-drive interregnum, and it was indeed Bill who got the engine ignited, Bill who drove behind me in his rusty Wrangler to the Volvo shop, a nail-biting half hour away. "Ma'am, you've got yourself a nest of mice," the guy said, when he called later that day. "Big nest right there beneath the hood. Not so uncommon. Creatures need a warm place to go. Got to drive your car in winter."

The price of the repair was hefty. The lesson had been learned. "Maybe . . . ," my father began to say, and a few months later I sold his car in yet one more heavyhearted transaction, a self-accusing hour: *if only*. We'd drive our drives in my Mini now, but my Mini is thin on the extras. I don't know where its symphony lives. There's but a minor display of elementary gauges. My father's memories are nowhere there, and the seats are small, forcing him to curl, with my help, when he climbs in, a little tight when it comes to storing the walker.

And so we drive less now, my father and I. We find less shade, less unfamiliar. Mostly it's errands but sometimes it isn't, and not long ago, on Father's Day, I picked him up from the curb and strapped him in. "Let's blow this popsicle joint," I said. "Choose your adventure."

He thought for a moment, but not too long. "The river," he said, and we were off. Down the curve of the road, past the long line of trees, over the bridge, through a tidied industrial patch, into the parking lot of a residential complex. There's a boat launch there and a bench or two, and in the near foreground, the south-running Schuylkill River.

Books ago, she was my story. She was, I mean to say, my memoir — this river of near-eternal time, this river rammed with perpetual middle age. I'd traced her life with poetry: *Were there language, I'd be my own lone letter.* I'd rendered her a seductress, a baptismal font, a creature of neglect and history, defiance and acquiescence, cargo and bullet casings, George Washington and Benjamin Franklin, a frozen wight being skated across, skated into:

Imagine taking a needle to the point of blood on your palm. Imagine drawing that needle around and around, leaning in on it, forcing an edge, tearing at the creases and the lifelines, the ridges and slightest hills that format your happiness. Imagine the skin giving way.

That's skating.

I'd used the river to speak for me on how it feels to be abandoned, how it feels to hope, how it feels to err, how it feels to be redeemed, how it feels to suppress your rage and finally unsuppress it, to take a firm accounting in the wake of a most-violent storm:

So I knocked you off your feet. So I took a look around, inside your basements, your first floors. So I went off, like a thief, with your June gardens. So I rose and you couldn't stop me, so I was brown and you hate brown. So there was mud, and for weeks afterward.

Think of this: I was kicking off your trash, spreading my wings. I was ridding myself of the insidious rats—their eyes like lights I couldn't see through.

My river flowed, she flowed, she flowed, she kept on living, she ran high and she ran low, she raged wild and she raged slow, she apologized and she hoped to be forgiven, she made room, on her last page, for love, for a river otter who was not finally:

. . . afraid of my complicated language, not afraid of my needs, not afraid of all that sinks or floats or ends with me. The bones in me, which are also seeds. The dust of distant life. The stories I carry, the color of my dreams, the weight of my confessions.

It was to this river that my father and I, on this Father's Day, traveled. It was to this place that we had come, and now we sat looking out, only talking when we wanted to, only watching for a bird or for some apparent life beneath the surface or a kayaker to come. A good time. Our best time. No problem to solve, just living.

I began to tell my father of some letters I had found, some words my mother had written to me in my twenty-second year. I'd never read the letters when they first arrived, for I'd been harboring deep hurt. I hadn't read them when I'd found them again, a few years ago, during those months of cleaning out the family home. I'd only read them recently, and what I'd found in them was love. Love I'd wasted years not trusting. Love that might have made me a purer version of myself. A more capacious, less guarded, less leaning-to-ward-intense self.

"That's good," my father said, after I stopped speaking. He nodded, wiped his chin, did not interfere or rebut or propose another version of the story I had told. And so, again, we sat, my profile like his profile, my tendencies like his, our ease beside the river a magnifying ease.

"Dad," I said, as the afternoon wore on, after we decided that, soon, we would curl back into the car and drive some more and find for him a milkshake, a classic black-and-white, a rule-busting Father's Day treat for the man who measures his blood sugar; we'd tell no one; he would not out me. "Dad," I said, before we stood to leave, "I've written of those letters that I found. I've written of me and us, of now and then, of broken things and fixed ones. I've written a book, or I'm writing a book, and I met someone, Dad, who might want to buy it."

The river flowed on, knocking itself against its banks. The river flowed on, dragging itself, trawling its past.

"That's good," my father said. "That's good. A book like that could be important."

THERE ARE NICE
PEOPLE HERE

"You must be . . . ," she acclaims me, as my father and I turn the corner at the village, ambling our way to the café.

"I am," I say, as I do now, my pro forma village greeting.

"Oh," she says, a smile igniting the prescient beauty of her face, a hint of mischief. She instructs my father to keep walking, gestures him away with the hand that does not hold the cane. "You go on," she tells him. "You keep going. This is girl talk. You can't hear."

My father shrugs, his own hint of mischief, and takes a few steps forward. I watch him go and take a few steps back. She confides now, a loud stage whisper. "Your father," she says. "Your father," she stops. "Your father is the *nicest* man."

"I'm glad to hear he's been behaving," I say.

"Always kind," she says. "Always considerate. Oh." She'd like to say more, I can tell, but lunch is waiting.

"Thank you," I say.

"You come back," she says.

"I will," I say. "I always do."

In the café my father and I ponder our culinary choices—soup or hot dogs? chicken salad? the shepherd's pie which appears to be missing the pie?—before we order turkey burgers. We move out of the line. We stand for a very long time as my father scans the dining area for the just-right table. "Maybe we should just sit?" I ask, after a while, but it's clear that my father is actively waiting for something, and that our waiting will not be upended by my arbitrary impatience, and so I stand there holding his milk and water, our utensils and napkins, succumbing to his timing; this is his home after all, his rules. Finally, his plan comes into view— two men, Len and Larry, elegantly crowned with white hair, also bearing, in their affect, mischief.

"Join us?" my father asks them, gallant with the invitation.

"Happy to," they say. And they are.

We pull out our chairs. We arrange our utensils. We look up at one another and begin. It's been a while since I've seen either one. We have some catching up to do.

"What's your latest best escape?" I ask Len, and he smiles, he knows what I know about him—that he's a man of ideas, famous for his getaway car and his exculpatory sightseeing agenda. He's known to announce, over lunch, that it would be a fine, fine day to drive to Philadelphia and take a Japanese tea garden tour, and who wants to come, and come on, then, we're going, and yes, however many can fit in my car.

"We've had some good ones," he says.

"Yeah?"

"Took the gang to south Philadelphia a few nights ago," he says. "The Mummers were playing a concert on the street. We thought it would be fun to see them."

"The Mummers!" I say.

"You bet," he says.

"But where'd you park?" I ask.

"Now that's the thing," he says, and proceeds to explain how he drove and drove until he found himself a parkable stretch of curb.

"There's more," Larry breaks in, Larry, with his dry humor, his gift for summarizing very thick books into lunchtime conversation.

"Okay."

"We went down to one of the country's oldest churches," he says. "We were given an impromptu tour."

"Interesting."

"Better than the lecture we saw the other night on fracking," Len says. "That woman must have been a government employee."

"You're just an activist," Larry says. "You're always looking for trouble."

"My father studied fracking," I say. "You've got questions, he's got answers."

And so the focus turns, and now my father is the spotlight, the light that shines on engineering, dirty water, science, the holes inside the earth, the terrible toxins of geological disruption, all of which leads to an anecdote in a book that Larry just read, which leads to an inquiry into the origins of the term *eggs Benedict,* which is interrupted by an attractive slender woman who stops by to introduce herself.

"Ask her her name," Len says.

She tells me her name. Tells me how she got her name. I repeat her name.

"That's quite an inheritance," I tell her.

"Only other people with my name work in strip joints," she says. "I've got nothing but time on my hands. Could be interesting." She saunters away. Style. Class. A chuckler.

The conversation at the table returns to interesting topics: Why is Camden a popular town name? Who was Alexander von Humboldt? From which dual-residence individual in the village might they score a weekend invitation to the shore? Did I know that Len's wife had once treated the GI problems of a very famous artist?

I try to keep up, but these village men are too quick, and after an hour or so we are caput. I clean the table, I retrieve my father's cane, we all head off down the hall in our separate directions, my father stopping at the memorial table to show me a photograph of Larry's recently deceased wife. "Dad," I say, you should go to the service," and he nods, and I sign his name to the list of those who will, two Saturdays hence, take the village van to a local church to celebrate the life of one among them, now passed on. We say hello to everyone we see as we make our way back to my father's room. We make small talk, decide how to spend the next hour or two, name the books my father might read next, decry the state of the world.

"You know, Dad," I say now, "there are nice people here."

"Yes," he says. "I'm lucky. I have made some really good friends."

| self |

There is rain inside my head, falling down, falling. On a day like this, when the finch that knocked against the windowpane has been left alone on the deck by the ants that had been feasting their way to her heart. It is Mother's Day, and I meant to take my mother flowers, but she is dead, and if I were to drive the pale peach petals to her grave and leave them there, they would rain away, and if I were to walk, I would just walk, my hair flat against my head and my eyes streaming.

Last evening, lying on the floor in the glow of an abjectly dubbed TV show, I felt my husband turn to look at me and I couldn't imagine what he saw. I kept watching the show; my husband kept watching me. What do you see? I wanted to ask him, but no translation is a good translation, and the rain had started to fall—sliding from the sky to the roof through my head, a persistent longitudinal spill. What do you see? As if my husband might do the work of knowing me. My self, contained in his gaze. My self, contained.

At dinner a few nights ago, there were plenty of us so we played a game in which our self, our selves, were named. One woman divided herself three ways—as the woman who had been decided for, the woman who was deciding now, and the woman she was during the two years in between. One named five husbands and so at least five selves. One annotated her resume. My husband's selves were himself before and after me—the exotica of his childhood, the suspense of his adventures, the radical growth during graduate school, and then a ring.

The game was getting harder to play—the Cartesian calculus, the Whitman tune, the grammar of parentheses and brackets. The self is woke and abnegating, line crossing and navigating, more-or-less list making, marked by the immediate and bent by the scene, the superimposition of other people's dreams, and I remembered the essence of a note I had written to a former student, now a man: But might your happiness be more than all the ways you work to make other people happy? Might you soon belong to you?

A game is a game. Play it in the moment, regret it afterward. I named myself a single self, fatiguingly abiding, a middle-distance runner running in her lane, still running.

[Did not say, My heart is wrecked by the pummel of its panic, the inevitability of its decay. No. I play by the rules of the game. I stay inside my lane.]

Therefore I am. Song of Myself. [me] Our words feasting our hearts. Our lives tracing the traces of our vanishing, malleable selves.

"Here I come to one of the memoir writer's difficulties—one of the reasons why, though I read so many, so many are failures," Virginia Woolf wrote in her unfinished A Sketch of the Past. *"They leave out the person to whom things happened."*

My mother is dead; she has been dead. I look after my father now. He wishes I would look after myself; he asks me to do that better. But what does it mean to look after yourself? Your eyes on your own eyes? Your eyes on your own back? Your words conjuring a self-knowing, self-forgiving self?

Might you soon belong to you?

On a day that isn't Mother's Day, the storm sky is gold-edged. I climb into my car and drive—suburban highway to country road to the senior living of my mother's favorite friend. I carry pink roses, pink peonies, pink berries, a book I wrote, its cover varieties of blue. "Bethie," my mother's friend says when she finds me, her cane curved, her spine curved, her eyes bright as glass, and I am glad for her, glad with her. I am contained within her gaze.

On the gold edge of the storm it rains.

She has prepared nuts and cookies, brownies. She has placed them on a blue tray and walked me through one room into another, where a gift my mother gave her hangs, my mother's words on the opposite side of the frame. She retrieves their high-school yearbook, she retrieves their Guyer Avenue stories, she folds and unfolds time, she is glad for the flowers I have brought, glad for pink. She is alive as she speaks of the dead, this favorite of my mother's friends.

"Many bright colours; many distinct sounds; some human beings, carica-tures; comic; several violent moments of being, always including a circle of the scene which they cut out: and all surrounded by a vast space," Virginia Woolf, in her Sketch, *said.*

Sometimes, when my mother's friend is talking, I am not walking. Sometimes, when she is talking, I am transmuted, freckled and banged, a jar of tadpoles in one hand, a piece of mica splintering in my pocket. "Oh," my mother's friend says inside that then. "Oh, Bethie. You always had that spark. Four, five, six years old, and so full of opinions, so full of knowing the thoughts in your own head."

The words rain through. Shameless, I need to hear them again. To take possession of the self-contained in the eyes of my mother's favorite friend. Her eyes on my eyes. Her eyes on my back. Her words conjuring the unalloyed proportions of myself.

"Bethie," she says. "You've hardly changed since then."

Might I soon belong to you?

There is sun, there is rain, the day can't choose. I stay too long, I'll come again. I take the nuts into the kitchen and the brownies into my pocket: her command. "For your husband," she says.

And now, as a mother would, she sweeps my messy hair from my face with her hand and kisses my time-lined cheek with her pink-painted lips, and says that next time, we will lunch, next time we will talk about the book you brought, this conjurer that I am.

And now I drive—country roads to suburban highway, silver to gold, moments of being and not being to a hill I take too fast, so high then low that I am dizzy at once and again unkempt. High, then low, returning to the house that I had left, and the rain that falls and falls inside my head.

CLEAN

Everything here now is clean. My pantry picked pure of rainy-day supplies, my crisper chilling nothing but air, my dresser sluiced of its delicate slips, my closet shorn of the diaphanous dresses I'd once loved to wear.

My life. My words. My sentences. My stories.

Clean.

The kind of clean I learned in my mother's house, my father's house, the cracked and cracking house. The plate, the cup, the spoon, the porcelain bunny. The Dumbo in a soar above the circus, in his blue hat, with a feather in his trunk, his big ears flapping on the pop-up album cover. The Dr. Dolittle talking to a snail the size of a boat in the blue-black grooves of a record. The Sancho confessing to Aldonza.

Those days upon days of stepping. Across the threshold and up and down the steps and out into the air. Those days upon days when I stood among the discarded until everything was bones and light. Until the house was a house built of graph paper dreams and blue notes, a hill's hole, a concrete pour, a system of frames, finishes, glass, a laundry chute that bled one floor into another and I was in the walk-in attic of split planks working through a final shelf of final things—my high-school microscope, my ladybug ball, the box of sand dollars I had bleached after a summer in the south, my Mary Poppins doll. When I was there, finding the last box and lifting the lid and scrunching the tissue back. Getting myself into better light. Sliding my glasses from their hair-band position to my nose.

I heard myself gasp.

I was holding my parents' wedding in my hands.

"Look at you," I said to my father, when he came to stand beside me beneath the bulb of light. "Look at her."

She was Elizabeth Taylor in *National Velvet*, only more stately, her dress crinoline and sweeping. My father stunned, in a white jacket, black pants, the auburn lights in his hair reading as auburn despite the faded black and white. I turned the pages of the album slowly, met my mother on her bridal day, watched her eyes fill, her flowers fall in a diagonal swath.

"Oh my," my father said. "Oh, my. What will we do with this?"

Yes. What?

You see how it was, learning clean. You can imagine the grass, yes, growing between the driveway stones. The spindles, yes, of new trees rising in the garden. The fumbling with that key on the very last and final day when it was wood and white and air inside. I circled through the dining room into the room where my mother died.

Looking up, I found a reflected me in the glass pane of the connecting door. I had lifted my camera. I'd snapped.

Nothing to do then.

Nothing but to return home, to my own house, and continue to clean.

Take it away, send it away, scrubbing and scouring and clipping toward sheer enough, light enough, naked enough, and when at last my own house had been rid and spared and picked, I fell upon the stories I write, which, it seemed, had gorged upon themselves in my absence, bred extra lines in the dark, decorated themselves in secret, multiplied as cells might in a warm petri.

Make them, I thought, virtuous. Make them clean.

Clean as an Alice McDermott image: "But it was at this hour, when the sun was humming gold at the horizon, or a pale peach, or even just, as now, a gray pearl, that she felt the breath of God warm on her neck."

Clean as a Bernard MacLaverty sentence: "If she was an instance of the goodness in this world then passing through by her side was miracle enough."

Clean as Inara Verzemnieks' seeing: "Sometimes a house stands still long enough to admit that it is abandoned, portions of the roof skinned away to reveal blackberries growing on the inside, the surrounding fields neck-high and riotous."

Clean as the lines of a Chloe Honum poem: "The fluorescent light / goes off and the shadows / fall apart like a cardboard fort."

Clean. Cleaner. Less and then more less. More condensed, more compressed, more precise, until my own books become chapters and my chapters become pages and my pages become just this one small something titled "Clean."

THE AGE OF INNOCENCE

What's missing is the warm sun on the thin creek behind the house where there will be kittens. The polished pebbles beneath the float of leaves. The jutting tails of tadpoles. There was a bridge, too, and the sound of the laces of my loosely tied shoes sweeping across the weathered wood. I quarried creek mica, pink quartz, possible slate. I filled the pockets of the culottes my mother sewed. I waited for the frogs to climb out of the mud of themselves—tails and feet and toes.

My brother was a genius—everybody knew. He had blue eyes that seemed to have no genetic sourcing, blond hair, which was just as strange in our family of brunettes, and a red-headed friend who had tumbled straight off the cover of the *MAD* magazine my brother read when he wasn't building model solar systems, model rockets, modeled math. When we played Monopoly my brother always won. All card games, too, were his; also checkers. When we put the needle down on our childhood hymns—*Windjammer*, Sandler and Young, *The Sound of Music*, *The Music Man*—my brother stood on the family-room stage and, with his lean, perhaps even bony limbs, conducted while I sang or danced or provisioned up a drum. Our mother cooking. Our mother sewing. Our mother fitting Styrofoam heads onto the puppets that she forged. Our father working. Our sister six years younger, four years younger than my brother or me. I had offered, before she was born, to name her Yankee Doodle. A first denial.

There was a hill and at the highest part of the hill there was a T, and to the west of the T there was a field, edged on three sides by ancient trees. The field grew fireflies. It grew red birds and black ones, butterflies with swift, unremarkable wings. It grew dandelions and then their tufts. Sometimes backyard parties would spill out toward the long sweep of long grass, and sometimes fireworks were lit and tossed and boomed, and sometimes I would run alone through that suburban wilderness, wild and free, and once, in second grade, they showed a movie of a girl who'd speckled out among ancient trees and never did return, would return, from the shadows and the wings, from her own wild freedom.

We played kickball on the asphalt, the boys and I. We paid a nickel a person for the circus up the street and charged nothing for our magic shows and I sold the beaded rings I made, door to door, until, during an afternoon stomp for beauty, a cat took my ankle by its teeth. There was a tree in the backyard that my brother climbed and steered ship-captain style and a set of swings with rusty chains and one day, swinging, I flew—the chain breaking, my arm shattering, my wrist always now missing a knob of bone, and also, there was a strawberry patch, like a green hem on a white house, and I picked the berries—red, hard, not sweet—and among the berries I found a dying bird, which for three days sang from the cardboard box I had lined with towels and set in the laundry room, and then it could not be heard.

There was a bench roofed from weather on the narrow front porch. I sat and watched the storms, my brother, sometimes, too—the invisible thunder, the scribble of lightning, the splatter of rain. On a Mischief Night when the skies were clear, my father sat us on the bench—my brother, me, my sister—to tell us that our grandmother was gone, and after that when I watched the skies from that bench I looked for evidence of souls.

On a sunny day in my fourth-grade year, a teacher whispered in my ear to hurry home: *Your mother has been hurt.* A long ribbon of macadam edged the deep backyard of the school. A gate at the ribbon's end hung off its hinges. A street curved along the opposite side of the creek, and all this way, in the surreal quiet of other children inside classrooms learning, I ran—down the path, through the gate, down the one street, over the creek, between neighbor homes where the kittens became cats, until I was banging in through my front door. It was bright outside but dark within. It was quiet, except for the sound of my loose laces. I found my mother on the family room couch, my mother still, not moving. My father wasn't home. My sister wasn't home. My brother wasn't, either. I was in charge. I was to—comfort? Fix? Reverse a history that had not yet been disclosed?

I was—to know?

It was a truck, my mother finally said, so quiet I had to lean to hear her. A truck that had run up the back of her white Oldsmobile with the friendly green trim while she'd been at a red light, waiting. She'd seen it coming. She'd heard the crash before it happened.

Missing the person I might have been. Missing how I might have reached for her. Missing what I might have said to her. Missing the field and the wings and the creek and the girl before she learned to fear the thing that might happen next.

SECOND COMING

Write it in the present tense and maybe, then, you'll change it.
Change the story. Change yourself. Produce your second coming.

You may have to go back to the start: 19 Burns Road, Ashbourne
Hills, the cul de sac. Your father works at an oil refinery. He
brings the thick, resinous lick of industry home, the smell of
concentrated crude oil and smoking stacks and the tankers that
squat out on the Delaware River. Your mother sits beside him
on the couch, a swoon of newspapers falling over his lap, rising
up to hers. She sits beside him, at the piano, the white light of
the bay window leaving them and that vase of exhaling flowers
in silhouette. Your big brother is blue-eyed and blond, he rides
a creaking plastic horse, he builds a city in the sandbox, he has
a brand-new bike and it has July Fourth colored streamers that
crinkle in the breeze, and now look at you, who are not blond,
who are not yet disappointed by all the words you do not have.
What you have is a feeling. What you feel is a balloon. It goes up

and up, with every day—your family so handsome, your family so strong.

The coarse, hissing pleasures of the sandbox sand through your fingers. The candy pleasures of the sun. The serene pleasures of the circle that your street makes, like the bubbles that your brother blows. You don't have words, and you don't need them. You don't have fear, and so you don't know how it abounds. You are just. Life is just. You are nobody but just.

Joy could be a word, if you knew it.

Trust, too.

Then a girl from that cul de sac, a neighbor girl, a girl you know by the whirring sight of her running all around, slices the streamers from your brother's bike, an act of violence, which is a word you do not have. Nor do you have the words to explain that someone hurt your brother's bike, which is to say she hurt your brother. You run home inside a tantrum cloud, with news you didn't see coming. You run home and some kind of pact is formed within yourself: You will be good, you will be righteously good, you will compensate for that girl's badness. You set your baby teeth on that.

A few years later, your father is wearing suits to work and your brother and you have a different house in a different neighborhood, a creek across the street, backyard trees, a strawberry patch, a sister, an address on Maple Shade Lane. You are in second grade at Shipley Elementary, where, it turns out, you are a lisper and a little bit of an outsider, a bit rigid, to be honest, not much of a laugher, not a girl to question the embroidered collars she wears or the patent leather, and the class on this day has been very bad; it has misbehaved. The class is to write apologies on newsprint paper with straight ruled lines, one hundred somber times: *I am sorry, Mrs. Kalin.*

You, however, are exempt. You do not have to say *I'm sorry,* because you knew the rules, because you did not break them, because you have kept the agreement you made with yourself: *be good.* The sun streams and the clock ticks and the pencils scratch, and it is lonely being well-behaved in the long lean of the afternoon, but goodness has its price. Goodness has its purpose. Goodness is what you have chosen, and so it is what you must be. The clock ticking. The hour in a stutter.

Now it's a rented house in Fort McMurray—your father's job again, the tar sands of Alberta—and your mother is walking the dirty streets with agitated haste to a booth where she can phone her failing mother. Your brother climbs the hills of mud and no matter what, the house is dirt-streaked, and the night looks like day only a little duller, and you believe, or perhaps you only wrote that in a story once, that, one night, in a shocking contradiction to the color brown, the sky dressed up in the green and red sleeves of an aurora borealis.

One day you walk home from school for lunch in this foreign place and then, checking the clock, you walk back. The playground should be humming; it is not. The lights should be on in the squat school, there should be people in the windows, there should be teachers. Nothing. School is out. School is over. You have missed an afternoon of class, and maybe this, in fact, is your first official anxiety attack, because you are no longer good, you have broken a rule, you have shown up at school after all the others have gone home, you were not where you had promised to be, you have failed the test, and this, as it turns out, is a brand new kind of violence, a kind that you visit upon yourself. You broke the rules. You are dangerously imperfect.

Follow the cracks, Casey Gerald says. Follow the cracks. Where do they take you?

Maybe the lying starts there. Maybe, because you've failed, you have to be another person. You have to be more interesting than goodness ever was.

Not the big stuff; God, no. Not even close. You'd need a more original imagination for that. You'd need a touch of charisma, a sensation-streak of gleaming deviance. Your lies are mere self-glorifiers. Your lies are medium-tall tales. Your lies are what might have happened, *but*. You lies are *notice me*. You get hot inside when you tell your lies. You tell them anyway.

Why not say, for example, that the boy who is braiding telephone wires into rings and leaving them in the dark tuck of your fourth-grade desk fashioned you a good six dozen of the things, when the accurate count might have been precisely two dozen, or imprecisely three? You can't remember now because you messed up all those dendrites lying. You don't know how many rings there were, but you know you tall-taled the story. Right there, at the kitchen table, while your family looked on. You made the poor boy look (more) obsessive. You made yourself look (more) desired. You made it all much more than it actually was. And look: Your family was listening.

Or why not say that you caught the flounder in a boat on the wide and roughened seas when all anyone caught off the dock that day was the blowfish, which attached itself to your sister's hook, her reel? Why not make the boast and keep it? Why not become the heroine of the fishing fantasia, the girl who hooked and spun and held that fish on its line for all to come and see? So long as the truth would not be found. So long as your sister wasn't near, you'd tell it.

Lying cousins: You Hula-Hoop for four hours straight. You cycle the block five complete up-and-down-the-hill times without taking a single breath. You win the spelling bee, you win the race, you are the highest jumper, the farthest thrower, the smartest one, the funniest. You're imperfect now, so what does lying matter? You're cracked, and the lying fills the cracks—it makes you something more than you know how to be.

You have blunt bangs, too-big teeth, uncurvy lips, scabbed knees. Your brother is the genius one. Your sister is the last. You are in between and unspectacular and (besides) no longer good, and so you riddle things up, you confuse them with your tattling elongations. Though you must confess that you have never gotten used to this—your heart still pounds and your face still heats and maybe your eyes still acquire their demonic glow (you're not sure) whenever you do lie. Easy to do but not easy to live with, lying is, and the lies are changing, the lies are changing you. You're getting older. You're weaving a web. The web is sticky, sometimes it catches you.

I didn't.

I swear it.

I'm telling the truth.

Why won't you believe me?

Why?

Sometime inside all of this you are given a blank book. You learn an important something quick: Inside the book you can lie and it won't matter. Lie, and it's fiction. Lie, and it's a poem. You'll water-color the blank pages first. Warp them with runny reds and blues, oranges and pink, that joyful color, yellow. Then you'll write your words into the watery swamp and watch them bob and float.

Believe me.

Believe this.

It's your uncle Danny, your mother's brother, who seems to see your struggle best. Uncle Danny, who is taller than the rest of you. His hair whooshing across his head like some deracinated wave makes him seem taller than himself, and it may look to others like he's come from Hollywood, but in fact he rarely leaves the Jersey Shore, where he lives a secret life in a modest split level to which you will be invited once. Beyond his thin screen doors there is nothing to be inferred: no trees, no grass, no zinging fireflies. Only the smell of the beach, several miles east. A ghost of a smell. Ephemeral and lasting.

Perhaps Uncle Danny cannot tell you everything about himself. Perhaps you cannot speak of all you are now learning to be true and false in you. Perhaps you are bound by the things you do not tell. Perhaps your secrets, in company with one another, are neither good nor bad.

When Uncle Danny does leave the shore he drives an out-of-fashion car. When he arrives you hear him—rattling up the hill of your family's drive, his back seat bulging with stuffed paper sacks and ribbon twirl, found shells and wrong-size sweaters, rose-shaped earrings in a little turtle box.

"Here," he says, when you're alone, and you relax into the truest possible version of your quite imperfect self.

"Here," you say back, for you have a bulging sack for him, too. Socks? Books? A tie? They're his. Also the magazine with the movie stars he likes to talk about.

One time Uncle Danny comes and you tell him you are writing.

One time you open the soggy book and show him the stories that you tell.

One time you read a line or two out loud and you watch the crinkles in the corner of his eyes that suggest, *I like that line.*

He says that your stories are good. He says that *you* are good. He tells you this in person, when he comes, and he tells you this in the letters that he writes, his typewriter talking to your typewriter. Uncle Danny reads, he encourages, he types his exhortations onto onionskin and post cards, he names the places to which you are to send your lies turned into poems and stories. *Alive! for Young Teens, Campus Life* magazine, *Seventeen, Young World,* the *Hartford Courant.* He's got it all figured out, your future. He's got a hunch that all the making up you've done has had a good and moral purpose. In all signature caps beneath his often-mistyped words, he writes IF AT FIRST YOU DON'T SUCCEED, TRY, TRY, AGAIN!

You believe the love your uncle has for you. You believe that what you've written down is not just good, but true in the sense that all good stories and poems must be true. You believe that you have rescued yourself with your words, redeemed your boring righteousness, redeemed your boring lies, redeemed yourself by way of the neuronal blip, the synaptic flare of the alchemical you. You believe that you have come into a second coming of yourself.

But when you arrive at college with your suitcase full of onion-skin poems and you hang them on the wall beside your bed so that you might study them, improve them, get them published in the *Hartford Courant*, whatever that is, or *Alive! for Young Teens*, whatever that is, your roommates' friends have a long ripe belly laugh at the poorness of your poems.

You walk directly in on the ridicule, the hover. You're trapped at the door, they're trapped by your poems, they cover their mouths, they can't stifle their guffaws. You step aside so they might exit through the door. You wait until you hear them gone, down the stairs, then rush to tear the poems from the wall, to stuff them beneath your bed. You don't try, try, try again. You enroll in history, calculus, biology, economics, law, accounting. You write theses on the dawn of engineering schools.

You don't know who you are.

Follow the cracks. Follow them forward. Pursue your second coming.

You emerge from college with a degree no one can say: history and sociology of science. You have not one single writing course to your name, have not sent your work to the *Courant*, have not told your uncle Danny about the sound of those guffaws. You become strategic with the real, become, like your father, business minded, forge ahead, unembellished, entirely pragmatic with all your matters of fact. You write about architecture. You write proposals. You write biographies. You write plans. You amass trends. You organize a library. You are good, so very good at this, you are fine—retreated and retreating fine—and then you meet a Salvadoran man whose stories can't be matched. Stories about near assassinations and civil wars and hurtling cars and butterflies as big as birds and a grandfather, a most elegant man, who sided with the coffee-picking *campesinos* and lived a life as big as a myth and looked precisely like his grandson.

The Salvadoran stories never deviate from the facts; they never need to. They are brilliant just as truth, and all you can do is listen, and so you listen, and then, when it begins to feel as if you will drown in all you do not trust yourself to say about what you dare to remember—the good stories, the lying stories, the sound of that guffaw—you buy yourself your own blank book but you don't watercolor the pages. All you do is write again. All you do is search for the you between the cracks of the life you are living. Poeming the deaf boy you'd mentored in the afternoon. Poeming West Philadelphia. Poeming the cat in a window in the Italian market. Poeming the mimes at Headhouse Square and the friend you'd come to think of as Dostoevsky, who is now no longer a friend because (this is a crack, you follow the crack) he tried to rape you.

The Salvadoran man paints. You write. The Salvadoran man tells stories. You write. In just a few months the man leaves for his next act—a school four hours north—and you spend the two years of his absence writing. Writing is your waiting.

It is later, when you are a mother, that you will find, in a Princeton bookstore, Natalie Kusz and her memoir, *Road Song*, a true story told true. You buy it, you read it, you live it, you can't bear the weight of carrying your deep respect inside yourself, and so you write to Natalie and she writes back, she sees you with her letter. You think of your uncle, his typewriter talking to yours. You think of the courage it takes to be anyone at all and anyone, especially, on the page. You think of right, you think of wrong, you think of a writer writing: *What with my own heavy responsibilities to family, work, and so on, I normally don't find free moments in which to answer mail, but . . .*

Writers write books, you are coming to find out, and some writers write back, and now, with escalating purpose, you become a reader, studying the books you buy as if preparing for a test, as if you think that the writers themselves might show up at your door and sit for a mug of hot chocolate and talk and forgive you for being righteous good and forgive you for your sloppy lies and forgive you for folding to the guffaw and forgive you, now, for not reading near enough, for not being near enough.

You don't know much, but you know this: You have to be ready, you have to know these books, you have to know them as if you'd written them yourself. You have to believe that, someday, you will be your own second coming. You are the classroom and the teacher and you read and then you write, and you will not publish a single meaningful thing until a small magazine with a stapled center reads an essay that you sent and says—after three rounds of editorial direction—*yes.* Your essay "Pearl" begins with something true. "Pearl" begins with dying.

The sun had already fallen out of its sky when we were given the news of my grandmother's death. It was Mischief Night 1969, and if outside the air smelled like cider and a band of pirates screamed for early loot, inside there were only the three of us—my brother, my sister, myself—sitting straight as perpendiculars and straining hard to understand.

Your stories will enter the world unguarded.

You will be unguarded.

Cracked.

Later you will return to Ashbourne Hills and not find the girl who hurt your brother. Later you will return to Maple Shade Lane and not find the rings that had been braided. Later you will study the maps of Fort McMurray and not find the school where you'd gone missing. Later you will go to the beach where your uncle lived and not find the house where he kept secrets. Later you will teach on the campus where they laughed at you, and you will hear the laughter.

You will use the present tense to resurrect yourself, but you will barely reckon.

You will write toward truth but even then you will be lying. For writing freezes what was in time, and time cannot be frozen, and what is here on this page will be left on this page, and you will keep on moving. Over hills. And through cracked valleys.

THEN I AM NOT A WRITER

If the terrible work of one's youth disqualifies. If a master's makes a master. If one must, on demand, diagram a sentence or parse the nonrestrictive clause or declare with a sense of actual authority that "we knew that gerunds looked like nouns but were really verbs because they could take a direct object."* If one must write literary for a living. If one must write writerly, always. If one must assert that there have never been, there will never be, long stretches of barrenness. If there will not be fiction when the truth breaks down. If the agency remains one's agency. If what has been written will be read, if what has been dreamed will not be crushed, if what has been promised won't be denied, if what has been lived will be finally loved, if the damage will not be collateral.

If one must be celebrated.

If one has been wronged and cannot prove it.

*Sister Bernadette's Barking Dog, Kitty Burns Florey

THEN TRY THESE
ON FOR SIZE

one— I built a garden. Viburnum, azalea, hydrangea, primrose, osteospermum, bachelor button, poppy, striped grass, silver mound, fothergilla bush, et cetera. I dug it out, I dug it in, I weeded, I kept a journal. Notes to self within the very early pages: *The bleeding heart is getting crowded out. The day lilies are taking over. The Russian lavender is fighting for space beneath the oakleaf hydrangea. The new purple salvia is hosting an iridescent spider and a web.*

The eye observing, the hands attending, the weather abiding, the blooms coming in. It's rather self-exalting.

Pages later: *The trees are holding onto their buds, a riot of whites and pinks and reds. My garden is so fleshed out and so complete, and the joy it brings is indescribable* (Were there better words to use? Does it matter, if you're a gardener?).

And again later: *Eight red crocosimia now in the side garden, near the deck, along the edge where the fritillary were until the deer ate them.*

The deer ate them. The spiders webbed. The weeds kept winning. My garden journal begins in June 2004 and ends on April 30, 2009. Just. Ends. Two hundred blank pages and a dozen built-in pockets and empty graph paper that should have kept my writing straight ensue.

two— I took Ikebana lessons in a neighbor's basement. I devoted myself to the rule of one-thirds, the clipped wings of Jane's tree, the bucketed monkshood and rose hips stolen from a mass of roadside vines. I'd gone weeks without sleeping and blamed the corporate work, the ghosting work, the anonymity of the words I was producing. I blamed being lost in the lostness of doing work I did not like, of being a mother of a child who was growing up beyond her, of being too exhausted by it all to be a wife, and so I signed up for Ikebana, because, you know, we do.

I searched for meaning in the bend of things and in the wide omnivorous eye of a bloom. I listened, my pen and notebook out. I documented truth. Thorns, we were taught, were to be avoided. The subject was to be turned back upon itself. Nothing is as lovely as the one odd thing. I went once a week, two hours every Thursday, when nobody could find me, and pods and kenzans and ceramic half moons were my tools, stalks and winterberries, pin holders, blades, and when I was done, when I had something that might have signified, I would walk the half moon with the stalks and blooms up from the dark, sooty room, then out the door, then down the street toward my house, where the Ikebana would remain in its defiant thirds until, by the next sly Thursday, it had fallen, singed, and died.

three— I climbed the stairs to a second-floor ballroom studio to dance. Rumba, cha-cha, and waltz. A gift from my husband. *Try this.* How I stood, how I sat, how I walked into a room and didn't possess the room—these became immediate concerns. Also: the untamed wilderness of my hair. In addition: the way I hid behind my clothes and failed their easy angles. Most troubling, perhaps: my tendency to rush, my feverish impatience with myself, my heretofore undiagnosed problem with the art of being led.

I had imagined the instructors leaning in to say—first rumba or perhaps the second—*You've got a knack for this.* They didn't. Dancing in the dark alone to Bruce Springsteen did not, as it turned out, qualify me for the cha-cha, and grace is not necessarily an elevated pointer finger, but still, for years, I submitted to assessments, acquiesced to leaders, persisted among the surround-sound of reflective glass, danced with my husband and danced without him, and learned more from a gorgeous twelve-year-old girl than I would ever be able to teach her.

I New Yorkered, ganchoed, promenaded, ronde chassed, rocked left, rocked right, shined, forward progressed. I even polished my toenails, and this wisdom I did learn: *Don't want so much and also want more deeply. Learn the steps so that you can forget them. Make the music smaller, bigger, better, tighter, looser.* I was taught to fail and left free to try again, and in the process, I learned some things about my own tenacity and hurt, my multiform needs. I learned the intelligence of real dancers and how they dance the thin line of knowing and the strange untelling of a song, and that dancing is muscle and moxie. Dancing is theirs.

four— I went to a community art center. I went because my husband said, *All right. Then let's try* this *thing.* This was before he was a master of clay. This was a place where the aproned instructors with peaceful artist faces taught slabs and coils and wheels, pinched pots and fire, shino on your shoes and a slash of weathered bronze glaze beneath your eye.

I learned to wedge the wet clay into a convex teepee with the meat of my hands and the strength of my back, small motions. I sat on the stool before the wheel locking my elbows to my hips. I threw the teepee down upon the wheel, stuck it hard, asserted my power. *Make the clay your bitch*, they said, and so I tried and tried until I could finally take both my thumbs, plunge them vertically down, and dig out an open place in the spinning clay. A nest. A volcanic depression.

Then I slowed the wheel and poured upon that head of clay water from a dirty bucket and pulled and shaped the clay and pulled and shaped the clay, my fingers at the three o'clock hour, until the rim would wobble and the center wouldn't hold, and there'd be clay in my hair, clay on my nose, and Brett the instructor would be standing there with his considerable height and calm, offering quiet words, reestablishing the elegance of the mud, finding a shape in the misshapen, whacking it with a stick, setting me free again until, after the clay had bucked again on the wheel, after no pin tool could rescue the rim, after I had crushed the mess with my hands and my body was a Jackson Pollock canvas—the muted Pollock, the grays and gray-whites—Brett would say, from across the room, "See that? You're growing."

BABY SHOES

They might once have been the color of cream. They're cracked wheat now. Not soft. Weak at the ankles. Crusty along the curve of the toes. When they were given to me, twenty-five years ago at my cousin's house, it was a raining day in a season of floods, and they had been buttoned together—a pearlesque button of the right shoe slipped into a loosened buttonhole of the left, as if the shoes had recognized their peril, the risk of separation in a storm.

"You should have them," my cousin said, and I abhor greed, and I took them, so that I tug at them now, I count the buttons, I wonder about the missing one, I wonder about the seams that stitch up the back and down the front in a most delicately unobtrusive way. There is no brand, there is no mark, just the gray fluff of accumulated dust in the slouching folds and I swab away the dust, and the dust falls—miniature thunderclouds—to the floor.

No evidence of wearing on the soles because my father never walked in these shoes. Once he was that young.

Just the other day my father was here, and I showed him his shoes and he shook his head as if he had never seen them before, had never noticed how proudly I have displayed them all these years on a wooden table that is so small I can't call it a table—more like a wooden purse with a stiff arched handle and four unsteady feet. "Dad," I said, "I love your shoes," referring not just to the cream that had become wheat but to the second pair my cousin had entrusted to me, which is more caramel in its disposition, with proper eyelets and proper laces, more rugged, you could say. And, also: referring to him.

I love your shoes. | I love you.

He shook his head. He is a man who comes from modest, and modestly preserved, shoes.

My mother did not save my baby shoes. In the months I spent beside my father sorting, packing, and relinquishing the family home, we did not find them. I felt something like shame that I'd lost my shoes, that they were not set aside for finding.

I have compensated for the absence of my baby shoes by buying the baby shoes of strangers. Twice I have done this—finding the shoes in flea-market stalls beside friable dolls with shattering eyes and mannequins wearing feathered hats and old LPs that are ten for a dollar. The first pair is five inches long, with three buttons per shoe, buttons that look like baby's teeth, and a stylish band around the ankles. The second pair is a Civil War special, coal black and serious, shoes like mourning. Here they sit, beside my father's baby shoes and also beside my son's baby shoes, because I have preserved those, too, because I believe a collection signifies.

A collection tells the story of the collector. A collection is a shoring up against the things that have gone missing.

So much goes missing.

There was a photo album in the family house that my father and I found while we were cleaning. A photo album titled ALBUM. Two slabs of wood for a cover and a leather-string binding, black pages thick as construction paper and photos held by photo corners that are the shape but not the size of cat ears.

A clunky, beautiful, falling-apart thing.

A tangible thing.

A graphic memoir built of frozen time and my mother's white-pencil writing:

It all began here.

Jeffie at nine months.

Mommy loves me.

And here's Bethie. No comment!!

This belongs to you, my father said, when we found it. *This is something we'll treasure*, my mother had written in a letter that floats loose among the bound pages, *and, I hope, add to, for it will become more precious as time goes by. I had fun doing it, and you may not think so, for it's not very evident at times, but I did restrain myself from being too corny. Anyway, those dear faces need no help from me!*

I have kept the album safe. I have shored it up. I abhor greed, but I've possessed it. Lately I've been studying it for proof of who I was—this middle child who grew up in a house of abundantly but incompletely preserved things. In the album I find my family before my family included me. I find my mother's first words about me: *And here's Bethie, No comment!!* I find my bare feet, I find my socked feet, I find no baby shoes for many pages, until, indeed, I am two-point-five years old, which is to say no longer a baby.

I am rugged in the photograph. I wear Dorothy Hamill hair before there was Dorothy Hamill hair and a smock and tights. I stand on a stool, a utilitarian kid wearing heavily utilitarian shoes. Dark shoes. Laced shoes. Scuffed shoes. Supremely unfashionable shoes. Shoes that would not have been worth saving.

But.

Wait.

Look again.

It's the child in the picture that my mother, all this time, was saving. It's the child, me, whom she tucks away. The child, me, worth safekeeping.

This is something we'll treasure.

Those dear faces.

I love your face. | I love you.

THE FOUR TIMES I
BECAME A TEACHER

The first time I became a teacher it was to build a community for my son. I had grown disdainful of the resume-crafting of not-yet-adolescents, the competitions and contests, the machinations of helicopter parents. I wanted kids to be kids—no first, no best, no better than—and so I invited my son's classmates into our home on summer evenings to experience the democracy of stories.

I read from "Casey at the Bat," "The Raven," *Tom Sawyer, The Call of the Wild.* I read Dorothy Parker and Eudora Welty, newspaper headlines, myths. I bought a five-foot-tall flamingo balloon named Fletcher, and I rolled waxy paper across the floor, and I laid out snacks, and I got the kids to work on building neighborhoods with magic marker drawings and words—characters, landscapes, dialogues. It was theirs, and to them it belonged. Or I'd say "bad-hair day" or "missing button" and they'd interview each other to get a story down. Or they'd be given a scenario to tell in first person and then in third. Or they'd listen to music and write the opening scene of the movie the music inspired.

It was dusk, it was twilight, it was moonrise, it was big. And then the parents would drive up and call for the kids from the curb and I'd stand at the door and watch the kids go. Mine. Theirs. Later I'd watch those kids grow up—see them around town, by the high school flagpole, at the grocery store. Some of them remembered me, but many of them did not.

Most of them, probably.

The teacher learns.

It was dusk, it was twilight, it was moonrise, it was big. And then the parents would drive up and call for the kids from the curb and I'd stand at the door and watch the kids go. Mine. Theirs. Later I'd watch those kids grow up—see them around town, by the high school flagpole, at the grocery store. Some of them remembered me, but many of them did not.

The second time I became a teacher, I wasn't sure. The invitation came from the alma mater where I had been an isolated, uncherished student. I'd been shamed away from writing poems by freshman-year roommates. I'd been humiliated by a missed allusion in the only literature class I took. Memories haunt. So do fears that you don't know half the things you are supposed to know since your name now sits on the jackets of some books. I had come to books in autodidact fashion, with a handful of workshops tossed in. What course could I teach? What were to be the rules? From what hollow in what bone was I to extract the necessary charm, the more necessary authority? I had no mystique and no defense against my own uncertainty and yet months of indecision melted into yes. I built the defense of an inarguable syllabus.

Then there I was in a puffy-chair room, teaching a handful of students what I had taught myself about the elasticity of memoir and the patterning of words, the misdirection of the ego, the virtues of the past tense and the seductions of the present, the memoirists who lie and the fictions that tell truth. Terrence Des Pres, I said, and we read. Patricia Hampl. Michael Ondaatje.

And when my son would call after every teaching afternoon to ask about the day, I'd hear myself telling stories. I'd hear the love inside my stories.

He is . . . I'd say about the boy with Adderall tales.

She is . . . I'd say about the girl who had left behind her early antagonism toward me and the class; *I think she's happy now. I think she's in.*

~~*

The third time I became a teacher I had been teaching for a while—constructing a new syllabus for every semester, no longer surprised by my love. I had made my peace with the certain fact that, with every class, my ideas about family would grow. I had succumbed to the ricochet of questions for which I'd only ever have half an answer. I knew myself to be one of those teachers with whom students shared their stories. She would have lost her mother. He would have lost his father. She would have lost her best friend—an accident. They would have lost their confidence and they would have claimed it back, and in their losing and their finding there was something I could yield, something I could make—a true, good class.

These things had made me, I thought, a teacher—existentially beset, perhaps, but teaching nonetheless. But then D. asked me to oversee his honors thesis. D., who had sat in my memoir class-room a year before. He had a new blue-rose tattoo, he was a master of "jawn," he had once been adorned by turquoise hair, he had brought to me a gift, a potted bamboo. His thesis would be the story of being a son to a mostly absent man—and sometimes we'd meet and talk and sometimes we'd ping emails back and forth and sometimes I'd ask him for more than he wanted to give in those proud and poeming pages, in those stories about cemeteries and the religion of his parents' cocaine.

I managed the tension. I thought I did. I was a teacher, after all.

But then I wasn't.

I said, to D., *Go bigger.*

I said, *Write past yourself.*

I said, *Push through.*

I said, *Put us in that graveyard. Put us there, beside your heart.*

Beside your hurt.

And D. disappeared. Just like that.

Would not come to meet me. Would not answer when I wrote, or sent excuses. Pizza deliveries in the midnight hour of shadowy neighborhoods. Family business. A hunt for seashells. A bum car. An accident.

What is self-recrimination? It is this: D.'s work was gorgeous as it was and I had overstepped my bounds and I had presumed to know so much, to be his teacher.

I am a teacher. I can teach you.

No. Not really. Not like that.

A week before D.'s thesis was due, an email arrived with the subject line: "Gesturing to the Universal."

I clicked.

I am thinking hard, D. had written. *I am writing and writing and thinking and trying to be inventive. I am trying to peer out at the reader. I send an attempt for your consideration.*

I read what he'd sent. I blinked. I hurried to find an earlier draft of this reconstructed scene. I read the two passages side by side and it wasn't just a what-happened-to-me story anymore. It wasn't narrow. It wasn't sliced. It was a story made bigger by the care he had asserted to look up from his page, toward us, a story that now sounded—resounded—like this: *We fear the unknown—the late-night creaks that resound from the basement as we try to sink into bed, the voices we are certain we hear calling our name as we make our way through a soulless alley.*

I paced the room where I work. I touched the head of the wooden giraffe that stands, a sentinel, at my window. I pressed my hands to the small of my back, touched a tear, let another tear fall. I became a teacher again, a teacher who finally understood that there's only so much you can teach. The excellence lives in the students themselves. The excellence is theirs alone to give.

D., I wrote, when I composed myself. *The evolution of your memoir (for it is, now, a true memoir) has been a most miraculous thing. I hope that you have kept each draft. That you will, when this is all over, when you have time, go back and track your own mind on the page.*

I have made some notes. Not many, but I hope you'll take a look at them.

You have done this on your own time, according to your own methods, occasionally allowing in but mostly resisting the old prof's exhor-

tations or worries. I hope some of what I have offered has been helpful. But this is something you have also learned through this process: That you will see these things through, in your own way, in your own time. That you are utterly your own person. That despite these four years on this campus, you know who you are, what you want, and how you will go about being you in the world.

The fourth time I became a teacher I couldn't remember not being one. The children in the house. The students on the campus. The honor thesis devotees to whom I attached my thinking but never my demands. The writers—some of them young, some not as young—who were coming now to the workshops I was teaching on a farm, by the sea, near a river. I was good at this now. I only cried sometimes. I only shadowed the writers through the weather of their lives—the wasps and wrinkled leaves, the spider's net in rusted chains, the abandoned boots by a rocking chair, the weave of strings, the voice, the mood, the stories that read like the long tail of a white cat swooshing by—because I loved them, because I knew I would always love them, because I was big enough, now, to love them like that. Because I understood what love after the deep immersion of love does and that memoir is the life wanting to be transformed and that memoir is the life we have been waiting for. Because I understood that I teach and live the only way I know how—up close and personal, and that there is no charm in that, nothing drawn out of the hollow of the bone. The thoughts are there. The strings are cut. The ideas float. Don't try to catch them.

And yet: When the writers of this deep immersion began to write to me after the landscapes were gone, left behind, after I had watched them travel far, after I had traveled with them—when they began to write to me about the other teachers they now loved, the teachers of larger insight, the teachers who *really* understood, the teachers of otherworldly astuteness and impossible lean, the teachers who had wakened them, I became a teacher yet again.

Say it out loud, fourth time around: Teaching is not possession.

Teaching is the parenthetical hold, the instant of discovery, left to the instant.

Teaching is structure, teaching is the room we build for the students who will come and then slip through—in and out, on their way to other places, other rooms, other stories, other teachers, other teachings. Your students will find you, they will watch you, they will ask you, they will read with you, they will escape you, they will transcend you, they will replace you, they will become their own instructor, the most potent person in their room.

Teaching is that. Say it again.

"So you will teach?" I ask D., who is a teacher now.

"Yes, " he says.

Your heart will break a thousand times, I warn. And you will have it no other way.

THE APOSTROPHE WIFE

I thought, Hell, I could use a little rescue. I thought, The parallels are profound. I thought, Wouldn't *that* be a story, now—finding myself inside another self, learning myself through her.

She would be my cheval glass. The slight-slant length of me.

I called her by her apostrophes—marking the omissions, naming the possessives. N. C. Wyeth's daughter. Andrew Wyeth's sister. Joseph Hergesheimer's extramarital squeeze. Peter Hurd's wife. F. Scott Fitzgerald's neighbor. Paul Horgan's friend. Peter's and Ann Carol's and Michael's mother. I called her like this because I called myself the same. Father's daughter. Husband's wife. Son's mother. And only after that, for both of us: artist.

You keep the first *H* silent when you say her name, but you say her name—*Henriette*. In the photographs she sits, she stands, she waits in the fields of Chadds Ford, in the snow of winter, on her wedding day.

When I put my childhood photographs beside hers, my wedding picture, the resemblance (the look in her eyes, the shape of her face, the misbehaving curl) is true.

Bill has looked at her. He has looked at me. Creased his brow.

He doesn't actually see it.

An arrangement of verisimilitudes:

In 1921, thirteen-year-old Henriette Wyeth moves from Chadds Ford, Pennsylvania, to Needham, Massachusetts, her father's birthplace. He hopes the move will be the start of a new career, for he has made his fame as an illustrator and he is desperate to be known as an *artist*.

In 1968, eight-year-old Beth Kephart moves from Wilmington, Delaware, not far from Chadds Ford, to Needham, Massachusetts, where her father will attend a graduate-school program—the start, he hopes, of a new career, one that moves him further from his days in the noise and raining muck of an oil refinery and in the outpost of Alberta oil sands, and toward calm, clean, suburban management.

In the 1920s, Henriette Wyeth—one of the nation's brightest girls, it's said, an artist in her own right, a young woman equally at home in the branches of a tree and in the high society of garden parties—begins to visit with the F. Scott Fitzgeralds, who are, she finds, outrageous.

Throughout her teens, Beth Kephart—not actually a brightest girl, a girl with poems on the wrong side of sentimental, a girl at home by the banks of a creek who doesn't get invited to many parties—

reads F. Scott Fitzgerald and Zelda Fitzgerald. She becomes Fitzgerald obsessive. Because they are outrageous.

On June 29, 1929, Henriette Wyeth marries the artist Peter Hurd wearing white satin shoes, a geometrical white dress, and a lavishly tilted broad-brimmed hat. She marries against the counsel of family. *He won't support you. How will he support you?*

On June 28, 1985, Beth Kephart marries the artist William Sulit wearing white satin shoes, a sales-rack dress, and a lavishly tilted broad-brimmed hat which she will regret before she's halfway down the aisle. She marries against the counsel of family. *He won't — You won't.*

Not long after Henriette Wyeth meets the man she marries, she meets the man who will become her lifelong best friend, the writer and polymath, Paul Horgan. They will speak nearly every week, the conversation never ending until Horgan, first, reaches his ending.

Not long after Beth Kephart finally steps out of the writer closet, she finds herself obsessed with a writer named Paul Horgan. The one letter she writes to him is written the week that he dies. Her letter is returned, unread.

Henriette Wyeth paints a painting that she calls "The Drowned Girl."

Beth Kephart writes a book that she calls *The Drowning Girl*. Until her publishing house declares its distinct dislike of the title and quashes it, as houses do.

Throughout her life, Henriette Wyeth has to decide: Love or work. Fidelity or freedom. Beauty or snark. East or west. Her father's daughter or her husband's wife. Her children's mother or her artist's heart—her palette or her paint, her feathers or her shells.

She will wait years after she marries to move to her husband's home in San Patricio, New Mexico. She will be gone when her father needs her. She will be mired in responsibilities that are not of her own making. She will charm, and beneath her charm, she will regret.

Throughout her life, throughout my life, throughout any life: consequences.

"What began it all was the bright bone of a dream I could hardly hold onto," writes Michael Ondaatje, in *Running in the Family*.

What began it all for me—this line of thought, this Henriette Wyeth obsession—was a second-hand biography, *N. C. Wyeth*, by David Michaelis. A three-dollar internet special inscribed to another by the time it got to me.

Wyeth because, as a teen, then later, I'd gone to the battlefield bulges of Chadds Ford and into the Brandywine River Museum, where the mad genius of the illustrator hung in a converted grist-mill. Sometimes the Christmas train would be running on its tracks above my head. Sometimes I would walk away from the galleries and stand beside the swaybacked windows of the museum to watch the swelling of a creek, aware that this had been Wyeth's land, not convinced that he was dead.

Back in the gallery for one more look, because I liked the fierceness in the Wyeth paint, the mad stuff of the artist's imagination, the scuttering of clouds over the heads of pirates and lost boys and arrow slingers. *Treasure Island. Kidnapped. Robin Hood. David Balfour. Robinson Crusoe.* In fixing other people's stories on his canvas, Wyeth had fixed the characters themselves—their oil-amber rooms, their shipwrecks, their plunged swords, their constraining knots and billows and torn apron hems.

Standing there I was already deeply in, it was coming for me, I took it: the terrible tapping of Blind Pew's cane, the toss of the sea, the breeze through a stocking tear, the V of hunted geese. No one needed to say it: Wyeth was a giant of a man, a king with a paintbrush in his hand, and so I went back and returned again to see what he'd seen and how he'd seen it, and the geese didn't get away, and the parrot talked, and if I stared at the brute man's cape for a long-enough minute, I'd see it shiver and lift like a wing.

Henriette Wyeth doesn't show up in Michaelis's book until page 162. This is after N. C. Wyeth has been reported on as a volatile, watchful child, a mama's boy, a teen with a facile hand, a young celebrant in the Howard Pyle school of illustration. After it has been made abundantly clear that the great N. C. was a less-than-forth-right fiancé, but that also, sadly, he was the father of a girl who died at just five days old.

Ann Henriette Wyeth arrives less than a year later, on October 22, 1907, her father's birthday. In Michaelis's book, Wyeth's first full words about his first living daughter appear in a letter Wyeth wrote to his wife, during a week of separation. It's April 1910. The house, he writes, feels "cavernous." Henriette, in contrast, is tiny. She appears unaware of the emptiness around her.

The next time Michaelis mentions Henriette she has a sister, Carolyn, and a brother, Nathaniel. Two more siblings, Ann and Andrew, will arrive in time, but even now, Henriette is a girl who knows how to please her father, a man notoriously difficult to please. A man condemned by fame and fortune, talent and despair, ego and poor confidence, generosity and need. Wyeth is an exalted illustrator. He wants to be a fine artist. "Like two men fighting in a sack," Richard Merryman said.

And what about Henriette, his daughter? She will have to be, won't she have to be, perfect? The pleasing thing, the obeying thing, the child who can anticipate and do, who learns priorities and performs them. The perfect child tilts inside the frame of the cheval glass and one corner of the glass crazes.

I craze.

Henriette's second childhood house still stands fixed, in the hills of Chadds Ford. The house that N. C. Wyeth and his *Treasure Island* built.

To get there, you wait for a shuttle just outside the Brandywine River Museum, where not only the work of N. C. Wyeth hangs, but also the work of Andrew Wyeth, Jamie Wyeth, Carolyn Wyeth, and Henriette and her husband, Peter Hurd.

You climb in. The door closes and the driver drives. A left turn, a right turn, a curving ascent, and Rocky Hill looms into view. Big trees and a channel of running water to one side. A long green tilt of grass. A low stone enclosure. Five columns like raised arms support a second-floor balcony and protect an open porch with shade. White shutters lie bright against the red-brown brick. A path leads to the great studio beyond.

There had been more gardens, more trees, taller grasses during Henriette's time. Robin Hood games and Civil War enactments. Horses and ponies and roosters and bunnies. Blackberry vines twining around fences, cows huddling in the shade, mushrooms fattening in their houses, Harvey Run sloshing in a twist below the meadows, and shadows beneath the wings of rough-winged swallows. The news arriving at Chadds Ford Station in bundled clumps, before the trains turned and hurtled back toward the brick and glass of Philadelphia, down the Octorara line, past fields, past trees, past vines.

Driven up the hill in the shuttle, in April three years ago now, I imagine all that.

Inside the house there is no vestibule, no hall, just an immediate immersion into the great room, which is white walled and perfectly plumb. An oriental rug has been thrown over the hardwood floor. A globe has been spun to a stop. Stuffed wingback chairs have their doilies on, the lamps are lit, the books are neat on their built-in shelves, the lid is rolled back on Ann's Mason & Hamlin, but the metronome's not ticking. Daffodils in a clear-glass pitcher.

Everything in order, preserved and safe, and through the north, west, and south windows of the great room an opal sun streams in, and any minute, I imagine, the Wyeths will return—N. C. in his linen knickers and wading boots, reeking of tobacco and rag turpentine and moss; Ma with her apples; Carolyn with a poulter pigeon tucked beneath one arm; Nathaniel with a block of whittling wood; Ann with a pocketful of penny candies; Andrew, sweaty and giggling, just in from another day of amateur spying at Kuerner Farm; and now here's Henriette—creek mud on the hem of her skirt, a curl surfing through her hair, paint like pale freckles on her skin, and a book, always a book, in her hand.

She has not yet met the man she will marry. Not yet battled her father for the right. Not yet acquired the new apostrophe:

husband's wife. Not yet moved across the country, from Chadds Ford to San Patricio, New Mexico—trading the lush green landscape for the arid hills, the song of frogs for the cries of coyotes, the overflow of rivers for a few expensive streams. She is, for now, a father's daughter, a sister's sister, a brother's sister, the daughter of a mother, too.

"No stepping past this line," the tour guide says.

You can drive, if you want to, to the place where N. C. died.

It's not far from Rocky Hill—a turn off the main road. You have to get out of the car to imagine the scene from every angle. The maroon station wagon that N. C. drove poorly at a snail's pace. Newell Convers, N. C.'s own namesake, in the car beside N. C. The boy is almost four. He loves Rachmaninoff Concerto no. 2, and though Michealis suggests that N. C. was in love with the boy's mother, which is to say that he was in love with his own son's wife, which is to say that perhaps the boy was not a grandson but a son, I don't know what's true.

It is said that the sun was sweet in the east in that valley on that day, October gold upon gold. It is said that N. C. Wyeth turned his car up this road, Ring Road, toward the Kuerner Farm and stopped the car to show the boy the corn being shucked.

That he said, *Newell, you won't see this again. Remember this.*

On Ring Road, the earth rises 40 degrees. At a high point in the hill it is sliced by the Octoraro Branch of the Pennsylvania Railroad. N. C. has stopped the car and now he starts driving again, just after nine in the morning. The strangest thing is what happens next: N. C. parks his car on the tracks. Or leaves it. Or . . . ? And the train is coming.

Parked? Left? Stuck? I do not know. But the maroon car with the artist and the boy inside does not move. The engineer slams on the whistle. He slams on his brakes. He curses a mighty blue streak, but the maroon station wagon remains just where it is, and the wheels and the wheels and the wheels keep coming.

The mangle of N. C.'s car in the mangle of the cowcatcher. The 143 feet of shriek until the train itself derails and the boy is tossed from the car and N. C.'s body has to be cut from the wreckage.

A crew working the line 100 yards away saw it.

The corn shucker's wife saw it.

The dogs saw it and heard it and smelled it and ran.

It is Nathaniel's wife who comes to hold the broken child in her arms. Her child.

It is N. C.'s wife who is driven, with speed, in a neighbor's car.

It is Henriette, miles away in New Mexico, in San Patricio, getting the news through the phone that her husband holds, in other words, on a hard patch of red earth in the tilted sun. She won't hear the train on its tracks. She won't be racked about the knees by the rumble. She won't see the gleam on the wagon, the gleam off the corn, the gleam in Pa's eyes—or the dogs, so many of them, smelling the blood in the air. The train whistle's blowing, scorching, flaring, and the corn shuckers have stopped shucking, and the dogs are keen, and the wheels and the wheels and the wheels are turning.

Henriette won't stop it, and I can't stop it, and by whom are we forgiven? Guilt is the face in the glass—guilt for the things not anticipated. Not revoked. Not fixed. Pregnant, Henriette cannot attend her father's funeral. She cedes the days to paint and canvas.

"When writing about family stories, in particular, I think everyone is at first possessed of a desire that every detail must be known, that you will fail if you do not nail down all possible chronologies, resolve all possible holes," Inara Verzemnieks once wrote to me, when reflecting on her work. "But it is impossible to know everything, and I think that once we actively acknowledge this to the reader (and to ourselves), when we signal that there are some things we cannot know, cannot resolve, this frees us to focus on what we can find, to use the small, quiet facts of a life to even greater effect."

~🌸

We toss two suitcases into the back of a rented car and fill the tank. By my feet in the passenger seat slide a pink book of blank pages, my camera and three lenses, my notes on Henriette, notes on San Patricio and the house of hers that stands.

"Ready?" Bill asks.

"Ready."

We've named our lady GPS Charlene, and she steers us on, through the June green of rural Pennsylvania summer, past the flecked silos, past the cows that slap their paintbrush tails, past the loll of pigs and the stands of fruit and the thin collapse of abandoned barn lofts, and over the line, into Ohio. Sia, Adele, Andra Day fill the car, and sometimes we sing along and sometimes we're quiet and often I turn to watch Bill, his face in profile—the cut jaw, the high cheeks, the man so many women wanted, the man who, for reasons he has never fully explained and sometimes, I'm sure, regretted, chose me—the countless and compiling imperfections, the tightness of spirit that still snaps back, the control of the control of the thing.

In the car, the music loops. In the car we sing, we talk, we don't. The hours and the miles fly by. The days, we hardly count them now. Columbus. St. Louis. Joplin, Amarillo. Hilly greens, rocky edges, signs for the Meramec Caverns and the Jesse James Wax Museum, and the St. James Winery, barrel houses and safaris and America's Sistine Chapel. Black cows, purple flowers, ponds the color of deep red clay.

Charlene steers us past and past and we are each, Bill and I, increasingly inside our own contortions—catching glimpses of each other in silhouette, in conversation with perfect strangers, in conversation with the land, the hours, even, the expectations we won't admit we have. We are inside the capsule of this cross-country event, this drive away from home and toward ourselves, toward what we're finding out. Inside the rental, the mood reflects the agitation of the miles, the shattering of the years, the re-remembered choices, until I am thinking of all the ways we hurt each other and all the reasons we're still here, and perhaps (but I cannot ask) Bill is thinking the same thoughts, positing our history in his version of the glass.

In Oklahoma City, the heat presses down, it swelters, it rises from the memorial of many vacant chairs, it suffuses us with deepened mood, and now when we walk, Bill walks ahead, and when we stop, I stop longer than he wants, and when we walk the streets, Bill speaks of the heat, of the hour, of this task, until I leave him in the shade of a garden and follow the sound of children playing.

We sleep then, and we rise, and we drive. Time is a silk streamer.

You try to hold on, but your fingers slip. In Santa Fe, I remember years gone, when our son was eight months old and I was chasing Willa Cather. Then was a cold New Mexico spring. Our son wore a cherry-red jacket with navy blue trim; I pressed my cheek to his head of thick black hair and that is what, in the town and out in the pueblos and on the road to Georgia O'Keeffe, warmed me.

"Why does the past do this?" Olivia Laing asks in *To the River*. "Why does it linger instead of receding? Why does it return with such a force sometimes that the real place in which one stands or sits or lies, the place in which one's corporeal body most undeniably exists, dissolves as if it were nothing more than a mirage? The past cannot be grasped; it is not possible to return in time, to regather what was lost or carelessly shrugged off, so why these sudden ambushes, these flourishes of memory?"

In the New Mexico Museum of Art, we find Peter Hurd's portrait of Gerald Marr. I study the parched landscape behind the pretty boy in the flamboyantly colored shirt. I think of Hurd and the journey he took—a boy in Roswell, New Mexico, a West Point cadet, a painter at heart, a bilingual charmer who came seeking the instruction of N. C. Wyeth, and got it, came searching for family, and found it, fell in love with Henriette, whom many other boys loved, too, then he got her.

But the greens, whites, and browns of Chadds Ford, the brooks and burbling streams, the hidden remnants of a revolutionary battle, the overwhelming presence of the charismatic and moody N. C. Wyeth, were never, finally, Hurd's landscape, and as soon as he and Henriette were married, he began to force his wife to choose between her land and his, her family and his people, her father and him, her canvas and his. There are no perfect choices.

I see Hurd's love for his land in his portrait of the boy in the pink-and-purple shirt. I remember his words to Henriette, in February 1933, four years after they married, when he has long been on the road, when he is desperate to see her, when he promises her that she will be the only one he'll ever love.

She is to believe him, she believes him and yet, in May 1934, Hurd buys forty acres in San Patricio for the handsome sum of $2600. The property will need work, and Hurd, traveling as he does on behalf of painting commissions, does not always have the time to turn the place into a home. Miles separate Hurd from his wife. He is tormented, he writes, by his wife's absence — tormented by the possibility that she has found a way to live (forever now) without him.

Back and forth they go, Hurd's pleas piling up, the unbridgeable gap growing greater, their undefended passion clashing against the ways they wish to live, individually, until, finally, in November 1939, more than ten years after their wedding day, a note appears in San Patricio signed by Henriette: She will come to live with him.

She will arrive by train. Hurd will meet her in the night. By the light of the next day she will find apples in the one room, litter in the other, proof of an unchecked bachelorhood in another, and the one single painting studio that Hurd has built for himself.

Their two children will be collected in time. Daughter. Wife. Mother. Artist. The apostrophes compiling.

During the hottest part of the day I sit in the shade of the hotel, watching the birds slurp water from the stone globe of the fountain.

There is a man across the way—compact and self-assured, well shod, a hiker's posture—who talks to me when he comes and goes. His destination, perpetually, is the mountain air. He comes here each month from Louisiana, where he leaves his girlfriend behind. He comes alone to walk the land until he finds something beautiful.

"Then what?" I ask him.

"Then I just sit there," he says, "and I look."

Inside the worn room in the worn boutique hotel, Bill is closing his eyes, maybe sleeping. He's been quiet here in Santa Fe—too much sun, too many tourists, too many miles driven, now, across the country, too many windmills with their metal arms extended, too many oil rigs pumping at the earth, too much silver rain falling in shafts of sun. He's cagey, the way he can be. If I say the wrong thing, I will know it. If I ask him what's wrong, he'll say that of course nothing is. But I know. I know that we've reached that place in our journey when he is yearning to be free—of me, of the highway, of the conversation we've been having. This is a destination in every expedition. Watch for the signs. Be on alert.

You go that way, he says, *and I'll go this.*

Madrid, Venice, Spoleto, Prague, Quebec, Vermont, Berlin, London, Juárez, San Francisco, Florence, Seville: Bill has (in so many words or with no words at all) said it. In the art museums, on a sunny street, at a train station, beside the canal, in the grocery store, in our tiny house: he gets his fill of me. He lets me know and what can I think except of all the ways that Bill was the freest man I ever knew before I knew him. How all his tales about songs in Roman subway stations and nights spent on Moroccan beaches and days on surfing beaches and weeks in Greece were told to tell me something. The moral of his stories is that he wrangles, he gets free.

I'd always wished, Bill has said, and how hard it is to reckon with the ways that I, from the very start, curtailed and contained. I did not have the capacity to abandon known things for unknown things, a plan for spontaneity, some small income for no income at all. I wanted to know the mechanics of untethering. I asked questions: If you leave this for that, what is the residual and where does the residual take you? What, in other words, is left?

Just us. The two of us. *We* would have been left.

Bill lies half asleep on a borrowed couch dreaming of El Salvador perhaps, or of the pretty Salvadoran girl he almost married, or of the North Carolina three who waltzed in one day to that Philadelphia architectural firm—swept him away, they were laughing. He dreams of packing only that which he himself needs and maybe even silencing Charlene and driving whatever road he chooses, stopping, setting up the tripod in the middle of the day in the middle of the mirage, in the air that even a thousand windmills is not stirring.

He dreams or half dreams, but soon he'll stand up in the shadows. Soon he'll open the door and he'll find me, and I'll be here watching the birds slurp at the stone globe, thinking that there is only, in the end, give and take and yielding, the bending of your idea of your ideal toward the one who loves you.

Off the Billy the Kid National Scenic Byway there is a loop of a road. A post office not much bigger than a Monopoly house. A polo field. A bracelet of trees in the near distance along the Ruidoso

River. The crackle of the mountain range. The sky with its threat of a storm that will not happen. We pull into the Hurd La Rinconada Gallery, which is central headquarters for the Henriette estate— her purple irises in buckets by the door, her wedding picture in the lobby, the sketches and paintings of the family on display and for sale. We are welcomed in. We are given the keys to the home where we will we stay—one of the cabins Hurd and Henriette eventually built for the guests who were having their portraits painted. I chose the Apple House when I'd called to make arrangements. It's over a bridge, up a dusty road.

We leave our car there. We are led by Denise toward the main house—Henriette's house—which was expanded through the years, refined, enriched, so that now, when we approach I feel hushed by its unexpected beauty, this "placito-centered rancho" with its bougainvillea spills, its cow bell like a lantern, its elevated stone guardians, its running fountains, its thick-trunked tree, its shaded gallery, its cool interior rooms, its glass orangery, its backyard through which the narrow river runs, the dark cows on the opposite side of the fence holding the splatter of late afternoon sun on its back, for there is, remarkably, sun between the black clouds. Hurd's hat hangs from a post by the door, his coat, a rope of chile peppers. Henriette's pots hang in the kitchen, her coffee mugs, a wooden spoon. A cat sleeps in the outdoor shade, and across the courtyard, past a low stone wall, near the rough wilderness of a rose bush, is Henriette's studio, the place the husband finally built the wife so that she might stretch her canvas toward his landscape.

The door is padlocked shut.

The place emanates.

Bill is somewhere else, taking photographs. I weave in and out of the rooms and back into the courtyard and stand beneath the thunderous clouds, but no rain falls.

Later, after we have unpacked our things at the Apple House, Bill heads into the mountains and I head back down the dusty road. Let it rain, I think, let it pour, but the clouds hold, the wind pivots. I turn toward the mountain range and see Bill up on a tall rock. Bears are out there, I think. Coyotes. Rattlesnakes. Elk and bald eagles. Herds of wild horses. Prepossessing boar. Fox. Rabbits as big as foxes. Bill holds his camera to his eye and steadies himself in that way that he does—one bent knee, one straight one, those gorgeous hips angled to one side, air in the back saddle of his jeans. If I were to call to him he would not hear me, and that, again, is the point, that is the sign of his mood rising. He is on his own in a strange landscape, daring the sizz of rattlesnake at his feet.

I make my way to the dark cows. I stand and watch and then sneak back through the arch, beneath the bougainvillea, toward Henriette's home. The cat hurries off. The air, for the moment, is still. I imagine Henriette cutting the courtyard toward her studio. Opening the door. Pulling it shut. She is thin. She is dark haired. She is agile. Her hair curls. She just wants a little time for herself before the next guest comes or the child cries or her husband rides down from the mountains on that horse of his, his watercolors and watercolor paper tucked into a pouch. His art first, and her art second.

I walk toward her studio. I cannot see inside. I stand and hope and take notice of the threatening skies, leaving finally to walk the back curve of a dirt road, back, toward the Apple House. I walk on. Open our door. No Bill. No noise. I sink into a chair and close my eyes and feel an overwhelming peace.

The shadows run short. The rain hasn't come. The silver colors of the hills are sunk into a deep gray green, and the canyon rocks

look new and clean, and the bones of the dead glisten like shells
tossed by the sea.

In the morning Bill and I walk together the trails he's already
tested on his own, these 2600 acres of mostly prehistoric earth. A
gravel road leading to a grass road toward soft hills of sage and
bloomed-out cactus, sudden yellow and purple flowers. Two fat
hares scamper up behind us.

There is fresh dark scat and the imprint of a clawed creature—
bear, I say, and Bill laughs at my unadventurous soul. "That's
not bear," he says.

"What is it then?"

"I don't know. Not bear."

We find a bleached bone with a heavy knob where a joint might
have been. Wild boar, Bill says.

"How do you know?" I say.

"Because I do."

I give him the fact, as he wants it to be. I look out beyond us. Broken
and rising earth. Silver grass. Yellow flowers. Scrubby trees. Clay
Bill would like to get his hands in. We are the only humans here.
He's happier than he's been for days, and suddenly I know that
this is a landscape he might have chosen for his own life had it not
been for me.

Husband's wife.

Wife's husband.

I meet Michael, Henriette's son, on the road. I tell him why we've
come, what his mother means to me, how I am chasing her in my
dreams. Go to the gallery, he says. See what you can see. He'll call
ahead, he says, encourage an assistant to take us down into the
depths of the place, toward Henriette's secret things.

We tour the paintings on display, the jars of color and photographs, the framed things, the Peter Hurd sketches, the Henriette
Wyeth Hurd studies of flowers and of people, the massive original
N. C. Wyeth, the letter from Maxfield Parrish to Peter Hurd:
"So you want to be an illustrator? Well now that's too bad, but I
suppose nothing can be done about it." Where the floor sinks to a
second level, a grand piano sits. I wonder who played it last, try
to imagine the songs, then follow the assistant to the room below,
where, as Michael promised, there are family letters, sketches,
scrapbooks, postcards, histories in their own inscrutable order.
There's a Hurd-Wyeth show being mounted back east. Curators
have been coming through.

"Tell me what you want me to do," Bill says.

"Help me," I say. He always does.

We pull at the drawers; the assistant watches. We take photographs; she gives permission. Michael calls, twice, asks the
assistant what we've found and none of us have the words for
it. We slide the folders out, open them carefully, wonder if we
should be wearing gloves. Don't stretch, crumble, tear, breathe.
Don't waste time. Look long enough to know what you're seeing,
take a picture, look again, and Bill's right here, with me.

Henriette is eight years old in a sketchbook, drawing fashionable flappers, a naked boy with a bugle, more girls with big hats, a polka-dotted dress. Now she's in Boston, learning to draw from someone who is not her father, hand-ruling lines to letter notes inside—*Upper arm measures, 2 hands, forearm 1 ½ hand*—working on the proportions of the Venus body. The stash of postcards written to her brother Andy from her European tour when she was young are stiff, self-censored. *Be a good boy, Andy.* Her husband's letters are florid. Her father's letters are gorgeously formed, conflicting and conflicted, out of order, read outside their natural sequence.

"Hold still," Bill says, as he tries to photograph the words of a father to a daughter. A father perhaps slightly envious of his son, a father remembering that brighter era in his life when he was the center of his family's universe, when what he taught his daughter learned, when his daughter still prized his land over her husband's, when she was a daughter first, and then an artist, and then a wife, and then a mother. When the family wasn't broken pieces in far-off places—Henriette's own children in a scatter as she tried desperately to put herself back on the trajectory of her career as a Wyeth family artist.

There's almost no more time left. I do one more gentle dig through N. C. Wyeth's letters until I'm holding the last one in my hand. The last letter of the day. The most important. The letter that Henriette's father wrote just a few months before he drove to that railroad track and parked his car or stopped his car or couldn't help that he was stuck, could not get unstuck, could not stop the hurtling momentum. The last letter she would ever get from the man who'd hoped she wouldn't leave the rocky hill that he had built for her, for her and her wildly ambitious family.

His last letter congratulating Henriette on her expanding family, her new responsibilities. His desire to find the right gift for the new child she is carrying. It is all right here in a letter contained, so far as I know, in no book. All right here, hiding in plain sight—a message from the past toward this moment.

Bill takes the photograph.

We invite the assistant to the Apple House for dinner, despite our paucity of offerings. She shows up an hour later, hauling watermelon and chocolate milk, her puppy happy to see us.

We sit outside, on the patio of the Apple House, watching the light diffuse behind the mountains, all the colors that Hurd and Henriette painted. The haze burns off. The stars ping in. We are the world's only people at the very edge of the world talking European tours and philosophy, architecture, the untwistable twists of family lore, all the things that people, in a quest for meaning, do with their lives and the loves of their lives. There's hardly any wine to share. We squeeze the last drops from the bottle. We spread the peanut butter and could talk all night, we will talk all night, we hear a rustling and we turn and here is Michael. He has a cooler with him, wine. He asks if we mind. "Join your party?" he says, and pulls up a chair in this place that he owns, uncorks the red, fills our glasses, asks us about our afternoon among his family's things.

"So," he says, and now his stories begin. The parts of things the books and letters left out, the parts of many lives only a son could know for sure. An occasion with Georgia O'Keeffe. Gossip on the visiting movie stars. Behind the scenes of Lyndon Johnson. The complicated repair of a windmill. The complicated lives and interminglings of Hurd and his cowboy-artist friends.

"Ruidoso," Michael says then. "Their honeymoon." And then he explains how, after that Chadds Ford wedding, Henriette already three months pregnant with the child she hadn't actually expected, Hurd brings her out here, to his southwest, so that she can get a feeling for his country. They spend a few weeks with his family—impossible. She writes to her parents—homesick. Then Hurd rents a cabin up in Ruidoso hills and they have time together. She paints what she wants to paint and when. He paints the same way, goes fishing. One day Hurd comes home with a couple of rainbow trout and finds his new wife with their unborn baby standing by a lit stove, a can of gasoline inches from the flame. He drops everything, goes running. Turns off the flame, hurls the can of gasoline through the window, sweeps Henriette into his arms, hurries her out of the door, lets the gaseous gases settle.

"It could have all gone up in smoke," Michael says. "Everything could have been nothing."

Anything still can.

"Their spirits are so big," he says. "Their spirits are here on the land. And so I take care of it."

It is so dark now. There are so many stars. There are bird calls and rustle and no more wine, now, in our glasses.

"When I first saw you," Michael says to me, "I thought you were her. The way you stand. Your hair. The way you listen. She would have liked you. She would have loved this. She would have understood why you've come. The truth of fiction."

We let the silence go. We let the birds sing. We let the dark be, and the stars.

"There's something we found," I say. "In the letters in your basement. Something N. C. wrote before you were born. A gift he hoped to send." I recite what I can from memory. I let the words sit there between us.

"Oh," he says. "I didn't know."

In the dark by the light of the stars.

In the early morning there is a knock at the Apple House door. Michael in his sunglasses. "Come with me," he says, "I have something to show you."

We're not actually dressed. There is bread in the toaster. We throw jackets on and we come. He tells us to meet him back at Henriette's house. He'll make his way in the truck.

No rain has fallen but the skies have cleared. I am foggy with the lack of sleep, the wine, the stories I have risen early to write into my book—don't forget a word, not a word—and Bill and I are quiet. He has loved this land and he will miss it. The benefit, to him, of my commandeering obsession.

We find Michael by the door to Henriette's studio—the open door. "She would have wanted you to see it," he says, cautioning us of the thorns on her rose bushes as we tentatively brush by.

It is a doll-sized world. It is muted. The light comes in through the many-mullioned window, a pull of burlap across the bottom sagging like a sheet pinned to a line. Her hardened palettes catch the sun, the domesticated paintbrushes, the tubes of paint, the bottles of turpentine and liquid Ivory soap, and there is a nest on the sill, broken, not craven, its inches being measured by a past-century ruler, maybe a century older than that.

Gold is a color in this room—the upholstered chair, the portrait Hurd painted of Henriette in a ballgown at the base of his mountains.

White is a color—the crest of seashells on the floor.

Wood is a color—the thin-planked floor, the crucified Christ with his crown of thorns, the little man on the carousel horse, the petrified tree, the hat hanging from the tree, with its pretty ribbons.

Blue, purple, green in the luminescent eyes of the peacock feathers.

Gray in the attitude of the stuffed birds.

Oat in the dried flowers.

Charcoal in the charcoal sticks.

Gold in the threads of an old doll's dress.

White in the candle burned down to its last inches, but we are coming around through the colors again, through Henriette's turning of the seasons.

Michael talks and I don't ask questions. He names the colors in her trays, the colors on the brushes, the colors hardened on her palettes. He talks about his mother's final days—her husband long gone, her family dispersed, her hours painting in this studio for the simple pleasures, the simple meaning, of the making of simple things.

Michael stops and lifts his arms. The remembering animates his complex features. "She's here," he says, and so it is understood, again, that where she is he will be also. That it is his great purpose to protect the adobes and arroyos and colors of the world that his mother finally adopted as her own.

Meaning here is what you hold on to. Meaning here is not the vanished.

We will go, he tells me, to see where she is buried on the hill. Beside her husband, beneath flat stones, past the raw-clay ditch where the rattlers live, under the changeable, paintable sky. We will go, he says, and then I will know everything there is to know, I will have enough, *won't I?*, to write her story. The truth in the fiction of the fiction of the truth.

"Write it," he says, and I promise, and it will take me a long, long time to realize that I cannot keep the promise. That I can—and will—write Henriette a dozen ways and still not find her. I can—and will—write Henriette, but I'll be the only one standing in the glass at the end. I'll be the only one I find, because stories, like the land, cannot be fixed.

Michael is about to close the door. He stops and then backtracks. He bends down between the soft striping shadows and chooses a palette hard with color, a brush, a peacock feather.

"Here," he says, and I don't understand.

"Take them," he says. "They're yours."

Take what you want.

Keep what you have.

More than a year later, home, I leave my father in the rehab center where he now is, where I now am, where I will be: responsible. I drive the half hour home, pick up Bill, and take him out for runny eggs at a local greasy spoon. We're going to take a drive, I say, and I, I say, am driving.

In my volcanic orange Mini, we listen to an NPR story about retirement-home romance. I reach for Bill's hand—his wedding-ring finger naked of his wedding ring—and say nothing, imagining us even older, imagining us in a village for the old. I keep us headed north and east, to the Michener Museum, where Henriette is newly on display. Her work. Her husband's work. Posthumous fame in a museum built on former prison grounds and named for a family-saga novelist.

We enter by way of the courtyard, pay, head down the hall toward the blue-gray wall that announces the exhibition: "Magical & Real. Henriette & Peter." The curators' words:

. . . it is the first time that many of the pictures on view here have been seen in public since they were first created, many decades ago. You might have thought you knew all about the Wyeth family, but there is more to see—as you are about to discover.

I have the arrogance, in this moment, to think I do know all. That there is nothing more to Henriette than the stories I have gathered, the stories I have failed to tell, but in the very first gallery, before the very first painting, a self-portrait circa 1937, I am brought up short. There she is. And I don't know her.

She is slender and dressed simply, in a violet-blue, big-button dress. The clutch of flowers in her hands is held high at an awkward angle; she should put them down, I think, alarmed, she should rest. Her auburn hair is swept back and slightly frosted, as if she had been caught in a summer's snow, and the truth is, she's not all that pleased to see me; she is preoccupied with the decision she has made to join her husband, at last, in his southwest. Her lips don't part, her eyes are sunk into the wrinkled flesh of her impossible choice.

Put the flowers down, I think again. Sit. Rest. There are others standing before the self-portrait now, and Bill is beside me, and I think of the words that Michael said: *You are like her, she would like you*, but am I? Would she? She has been caught, mid-flowers, off guard, busy and in between, and I am embarrassed by my intrusion, studying her face for my own face. A sign. A tremble. The smallest inflection of recognition. But she is deep inside her own story. She is not responsible to me.

"Take my picture?" I say to Bill, handing him my phone and standing beside Henriette, where the frame divides us. The museum light eclipses. The photo contains no hint of a resemblance. We are two women standing in our own spaces.

In the well of this first room there are self-portraits in proximity to self-portraits. In every one she is a different Henriette. In one pencil sketch of 1924 she glares at something off to her left, her right eyebrow lifted in a hard arch, her hair vague once it falls below the abrupt line of her jaw. In an oil on canvas of that same year, half her face is barely there—maybe it was never finished, maybe she scrubbed it off, but either way there are few fixed edges, few clues as to where she begins and where she ends. Two years later, in a painting from her Pennsylvania Academy of Fine Arts studies, she has turned her head over the opposite shoulder, bobbed her hair with asymmetric self-assurance, accentuated the angle of her nose, and made a proclamation of her neck, in stern contrast with her white collar, while in 1928, her hair is gold and soft and her face is round and soft, and she doesn't mind, at last, looking at us.

I do not mind being seen.

There is an infinitude of Henriettes, I decide. An infinitude of us. Declared. Unfinished. Defiant. Unrevealed.

"Take my picture," I say again to Bill, fixing myself beneath the harsh lights and outside her frames, and in every photograph, I am only myself and she is the canvas, there, in the tight coil of the first gallery room, there, in the wide, bright hallway of the second, there, around the corner, where the painted irises grow.

There is another tuck of a room where Henriette's paintings hide. I step inside. Here are *Chinese Doll* and *Drowned Girl*. Here are images of fantasia, swirl, girls like dolls, lifelike dreams, and on the solitary bench before a canvas called *The Picnic* sits a woman, alone, mesmerized.

The canvas is big, mural-sized. It is of three girls together in a garden, though you could also say that it is of three girls alone, three who share nothing but a moonlit landscape. One like a princess, one like a mermaid, one far off to one side, only her head bobbing to the surface.

The woman, the real woman on the bench, is also, I think, mesmerized—her bright hair brushed to one side, her dark slacks and shirt in purposeful contrast to the floral scarf she wears, big flowers, muted colors, a pattern Henriette might have painted into one of her backgrounds.

"What are you thinking?" I ask her. "About *The Picnic*."

"Oh," she says. "So beautiful."

I detect her accent. She smiles. She says, "I have been here before."

"Here?" I say.

"Yes," she says. "A few days ago. And I'll come back again."

She feels something, she says, something for Henriette. She had never heard of this painter before, but now she thinks that perhaps Henriette has been waiting for her. She is a painter, too, she tells me. A Russian who moved here years ago.

"And you?" she says.

"A writer," I say. "I've been trying to write Henriette's story. I've been thinking that if I wrote her story I could write my own."

She wants to know more, and I tell her. We walk the small room again, stand before my favorite photograph of Henriette. She has not married yet. She has been painting.

"Beautiful," the woman says, and I agree, and now I take the Russian painter's photograph with my phone, in front of *The Picnic*, a picture I will send her later, tomorrow, send to Michael, too, show my husband when he finds us.

We sit together on the bench and she shows me, on her phone, her own bold landscapes—cleft-palate cliffs, rock slopes, sun breaks. She scrolls. Lately, she says, her paintings have undergone a strange migration—the mountains more like giant shells, the skies more like feathers, imagery she cannot quite explain to herself but she is certain Henriette would understand, and now here comes Bill, and still we sit here, talking. One woman in the early thrall of Henriette, one woman emerging. I tell her about the journey we made, about the hills of San Patricio, about the peace in the air of Henriette's studio, about the thousands of acres of silence.

"You should go," I say. "She is there," I say. "You can feel it."

We leave the small room for the wide hall. We revisit the paintings we have already studied. She tells me what she sees and I tell her what I think and Bill heads off for Peter's gallery, comes back, heads off again, until it's clear that it's time for both of us to go.

We leave through the door by which we came. The curator's warning: *You might have thought you knew all about the Wyeth family, but there is more to see—as you are about to discover.* I stop one more time at the self-portrait with the flowers. I catch the museum guard's eye.

"What do you think?" I ask.

"Of her?" he says.

I nod.

"Well," he says. He stalls. "Well."

I step closer to him. I wait.

"It's just not clear," he says, looking up toward the flower portrait, "why you'd paint yourself that way."

"What way?"

"So plain," he says. "So ordinary."

WHY I NEVER LEARNED TO SPEAK YOUR LANGUAGE

Because I have hardly learned to speak my own.

CAW

(in the manner of Elizabeth Bishop)

We were in a garden, a hundreds-of-acres garden. Boxwoods and camellias and fields upon tall grasses, bloom fortresses and tree houses, a conservatory of glass halls and orchid silks—and the sky was gray and there were holly colors and what if the afternoon went dark with dusk before we might not find him?

I close my eyes and time is not distance, and my son, my one dark-haired son with a mind for hard facts and an imagination I am still imagining, is lost somewhere in the hundreds, behind what Yellow Cucumber Magnolia or Shumard Oak, what Gloryblower or Bigleaf, what Italianate or otherwise. I am running, calling out to the easy strollers, the mothers and the fathers who had not bent to smell into the seduction of a flower and, in that moment, turned their back on the greater love.

A boy, I say. *A dark-haired boy.*

I run through the garden theater, between the garden beds, along the garden pool, toward the fields upon tall grasses, calling his name, anguishing for a rustle in the seedy stalks, the caw of a signaling crow. Running east until there is no more east, just west or north or south. I turn back on the diverging trails, the strangers who have not seen the dark-haired boy. The garden people in their garden carts are looking for him now, my husband and his brother are looking, the sky is falling, and the paths are arteries when what we seek are veins, the inhale and the exhale of the trees as they breathe, and I caw, I caw, I caw.

In Venice, at the Biennale (another year, a separate time), I have been photographing my son inside a silhouette of blue, inside sheets of mylar words, on the right side of a stilted arc, not in approximation to the viscous screed when I lose him in a room so midnight hued you have to touch your way through. My panic is more practiced now, a precipitating trigger, and through the interregnum of art I run, out into the sinking city toward the canal and the blind bend of the alleys, then back into the art—blue room, black room, white room, red—and when my husband runs through the galleries, I run the canal, and when he runs the canal I run the art, and it is closing hour soon, and the Biennale empties of its crowd.

Once, in a move, I lost the single box of things that bore the memory stings of photographs—the European masks and porcelain dolls and gifts a father brings a daughter when both are young and won't be that way again. It has been twenty-five years and I am still looking for that box, still awake at night with the loss of the things that had me in them, and I know they are gone, and I am searching.

Once, on my twenty-first birthday, I lost my mother's love; I being, she said, the daughter she wished she had not had; she said it on the phone, she said it to her friend, and I was sitting on the stairs, and so I heard, and so, despite all countervailing measures and other marques of maternity, I believed her, losing the idea of myself as cherishable, losing the possibility of being, as myself, enough, I would never be enough, I'm not enough. I am twenty-one years old, and time is not distance.

Once I lost the argument and then the friend, the hope and then the nuance, the narrative and then the story. I lost the sole of my shoe in the footsteps of a millionaire and my husband's attention to another's laugh and my ability to understand to chronic inability and my promise to the way I broke it. I lost the only pearl my grandmother wore. I lost the turtle earrings and the sapphire pendant and the diamond in the ring beside my wedding band. I lost the tango on the stage. I lost the things I should have said. I lost my honor and my moment and my own middle distance. I lost a day and then a moon and then the woman in the photograph with eyes so huge and skin so close to the bone it sleeved her muscle (*Write* it!), but in the garden at dusk, in the city of sink, I found, I found my son.

WHEN HE GOES

When he goes to El Salvador, he goes.

To the myth of the backward running feet, to the butterflies with bird wings, to his mother, in her bed, waiting. To the streets and the walls that siphon the streets and the houses behind the walls. Finding the door. Closing it.

When he is seen in his country, he does not see me. Two countries make him two men, and marriage is a sideways slide.

Meanwhile, the house here is quiet. Meanwhile, I watch the Pennsylvania sky through the bedroom windows—the dark arms of the pliable trees against the darkening sky, the black too thick for insect song, the champagne break of dawn. Meanwhile, I sweep the spiders from the ceiling and watch them twist and snap off their delicate strings.

Two days ago, I woke to the screams of American birds and went to the window and saw through the drag of yard shadows a giant turtle, a true dinosaur of a thing moving from no pond to no stream. It was never quite on balance as it careened beneath the screams. It was not at home in its muddy shell. There was no one here to tell the story to, and besides, there are plenty of turtles in El Salvador, there are many, my husband says, beautiful things in his heartbreak country. Still.

They hold his hand as he speaks. They rhythm back through time to the time when he was always there among them, glossed with mischief and unusual for how he could paint and how he could sing and how he did not need their love and therefore claimed it. Beyond the ruined streets, behind the walls, their history is his history, and he is home.

Last night, Independence Day, I stood at the window and strained to see the flames tossed up beyond the trees. I only smelled the smoke. I only heard the artillery of the ascent, the bang of color, until the percussive invisibility became a metaphor I might have said out loud, but words exclaimed in an empty room are pure self-conscience, the narcissist's folly.

I watch films when he is gone; he doesn't know. I watch a young man with autism go up and down the aisles of a country church saying, *I am so happy to see you, I am so happy*, and I feel the bones around my heart crack, but don't report the injury. The neighbor with whom I once warred comes to the edge of the grass to make confessions, and that I am glad for this is nothing my husband would intimate, for he is in the swell of his own first world, the hot gardens of bird call, the crowd of people I amend mostly for the unsummed totals of their anecdotes.

His El Salvador is his first hero, his first sex, his first impulse, the instincts to which he returns, the source of the charcoal figures he draws, the mystery that, through decades now, I've more than loved, I've boasted of, I've fought against and for, and who am I to imagine his El Salvador, or to imagine he might imagine all this silence when he's gone.

The sky clears itself of the smoke in the dawn.

The turtle hides in its shell like a stone.

WHEN HE COMES BACK

I read what you wrote, he texts. *I think it's a poem and it's very powerful but I do see you when I'm here. I had some time to think "amid the noise and haste"—just to the edge though, not too far that I couldn't pull myself back quickly. It is overwhelming to manage thoughts when there is so much input. But I'm at the gate now, happy that I'll see you soon. Love you and missed you. I did.*

I buy cherries. I buy grapes. I buy plums and Boursin cheese, sliced bread, ice cream, the usual. I drive to the airport and now he is home for this midnight feast, but he barely eats for he has barely eaten during the week he's been gone, he is not hungry for any of this. He is hungry with the stories he starts to tell, and I am hungry with my listening, and so we talk all night, and then he goes to sleep, and somewhere out there the turtle inside its stone shell breathes.

The next day the house is hot. The next day he returns to the room where he sketches, and in time it grows so quiet that I worry. I stand from this desk, leave my work room for his and find him there—folded into the half couch, one hand over his heart, his head turned toward the pillows.

The freckle on his Salvadoran face is the dark island I still study.

COLLISIONS

When I remember it, I remember wrong; I remember versions. I hit the truck or the truck hit me. I saw it coming or I didn't. I'd forgotten how to stop, I never knew how to stop, I should not have been rollerblade-soaring down the neighborhood hill. All I wanted was my freedom.

By the time I dragged my body home it was a foreign color. A moon was rising high on my thigh, an astral rock that, all these years on, is glowing.

It frightens me.

It is me.

When I was struck again, I was only walking—early on my way to a teaching day on an urban campus, headed for the train. There was ice on the roads and the signs and the wires. The sun on that ice was blinding. At the four-lane crossing, the only car I saw had stopped to wave me forward. Into the dazzle of the road I stepped. In memory, I still do not see the second car. I only hear the shattering. Then vision returns: The busted side mirror of the car on the asphalt. The commotion of books. The far-off toss of the hat that had been ripped from my head. The old woman beside the old man in that old car, praying.

The train shivered in. I collected what could be collected and abandoned my asundered hat and jagged toward the platform, hardly breathing. The train doors opened then closed on the crowded heat and the car rocked and suburbia blurred and my left arm was now too thick for the sleeve of my shirt, the sleeve of my sweater, the sleeve of my jacket; my left arm was detonating. *I have been hit*, I confessed to a stranger. Eight stops east, we left the heat of the train for the cold of the city. The stranger flagged a taxi. She slid in beside me and we sped, and now, in the emergency room: X-rays, a sling, codeine, a three-hour wait for my release. *Release me.* I walked the campus to the Victorian room with the damaged velvet curtains and taught the students who had been waiting, the students I called my Spectaculars, for nothing had been broken.

All of this arises in the horizontal now, on a crooked page, during a morning's bout with vertigo. All these words are suddenly here, drawn up from the unguarded well of my remembering, and now another thought stirs—unruly, undisciplined, implicating: *I was my mother's first-born daughter, but not her favorite*. It is a single inapposite assertion, an eruption from the middle child who is far too old to be haunted by former disequilibria and secret exclusions, the history of preference for the second daughter, but here I am—ridiculous and entrenched—writing the words down on the page.

Vertigo tilts perspective. I stare at the words *but not her favorite* and the story pivots. The story is no longer me and my vehicles but my mother and hers. We called it an accident, but it wasn't. What happened to my mother involved thieves—a premeditated snatch of her purse while she was zippering herself into a fashionable choice in a Boston dress shop. The hands reached beneath her changing-room door. The feet ran. There was jewelry in my mother's purse, there were keys, there was pride, and she went running, shoeless, after the assailants into the street, where the getaway car was revving. She was nearly there. She inhaled and stretched. She was knocked to the ground and the car accelerated over thighs, knees, feet, over neurons, axons, over electrochemistry.

I was a college freshman when my father brought my mother home from Boston. I returned to the house each weekend to sit by the couch where she lay. I brought Termini Brothers biscotti, train-station flowers, F. Scott Fitzgerald, medical news on crush and chronic pain and transcutaneous electrical nerve stimulations and bags of ice and glass bells and glass apples and glass angels and anything, anything to short-circuit her short circuits, but my mother had been thieved.

After I hit the truck or the truck hit me, I stopped roller-blade-soaring toward freedom. After my arm sliced the side mirror from an old man's car, I could barely leave one side of the road for the other, and crossing stops me still: the hyperventilating double takes, the east-west calculations, the curbside stranding, that mark on the asphalt where it happened. After my mother was shoved beneath the wheels of the getaway she was permanently rearranged—new messages sent through new pulse pathways toward a self-defending brain.

She missed dancing the Charleston.

She missed walking the beach.

She missed bike rides and tennis games and easy sewing and sleep and unswollen knees and the first-born daughter who, once, had had no need to fix her, who, once, had not asked after pain she couldn't explain, who, once, had not been cureless, clueless, even. Week after week.

Months.

Years.

Time is a glass arrow. Time is the ice on the telephone wire, the distortion of the gleam. Now onto this crooked page I am writing my twenty-first birthday. I am placing myself on the fourth step of the hallway stairs in the house with the couch while my mother is on the phone in the kitchen talking to her best friend. Her nerves misfire, and her thighs tumefy, and her pain is the pain I cannot cure, and she is saying: *Beth is the daughter I wish I'd never had. Beth is too much trouble.*

If saying is the wreck of a thing, so is not unhearing.

In the long afterward—my marriage, my child, my home, my words—my mother and I bought each other many things. She bought me winter coats and reading lamps, shelves and volumes, necklaces and rings. I bought her porcelain shoes and pepper shakers, Humpty Dumpty figurines, more F. Scott, glass hearts, glass apples, glass wings.

The things were hieroglyphs and intercessions. The things were the wedge between. The things accounted for the fact that I had never told my mother what I had heard, had not explained my own self-defending brain, had left her in the dark regarding my emotional retreating.

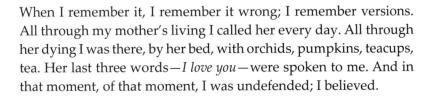

When I remember it, I remember it wrong; I remember versions. All through my mother's living I called her every day. All through her dying I was there, by her bed, with orchids, pumpkins, teacups, tea. Her last three words—*I love you*—were spoken to me. And in that moment, of that moment, I was undefended; I believed.

Still, in this long morning, this afternoon, now, of vertigo, the old wounds rise, astral. The old wounds turn a story twice, and so I stand from the bed and steady myself and head downstairs to the box where I have been keeping a handful of my mother's letters, most of them written in my twenty-second year. I have had these notes for many years now, and I have never read them.

Dear Betsy,

I remember when I was 22—all day I said to anyone who would listen, "Today is the 22nd of May and I'm 22." Wasn't I clever? But I suppose that, in a way, is not all as dumb as it sounds. Perhaps that is one of life's mysteries—to find a near perfect balance between life's simplicities and life's mysteries.

Now last night, when sleep was reluctant to rest on any pillow, I thought of beautiful things I could say to my beautiful 22-year-old—now, however, it just seems that I don't want to be clever or wordy—I just want to tell you how much I love you—Dad and I—and how pretty your little brown head of curls is. Your smile is an instant frown remover and your talents abound. Mostly, we just love you.

Dear Betsy:

May the wisps of childhood-like occupations always remain to replenish, uplift, and delight you. They should always be a tool of your craft.

This gift required the convergence of all three of our ideas—what would please Betsy most? This is our collective worldly interpretation. Were we close to the mark?

Your father and I want to tell you that whatever the weights and hollowness of attending Penn, you did do it on your own intellectual magna-cum-laude terms. More importantly, however, you did it on your own moral terms. No one can underestimate that achievement. Dad and I are suitably proud of you for that.

Dear Betsy:

I think I've jumped around a lot, but images don't always assemble themselves in a rational line. Feelings are brittle, porcelain-like. They crack, they chip, and sometimes break into smitherins. (Now there's a word I've heard used many times and don't think I've ever seen. It's a word, isn't it?) Sometimes a chip doesn't matter. But sometimes the finest artisan can't repair the damage and it must be discarded . . . The summer has been such a maze. Trying to rationalize you there, us here.

Dear Betsy:

You were once an etherial creature.

Smithereens is a word, Mom, yes.

Your *smitherins* break me.

I saw it coming, or I didn't. I heal myself with versions, or I won't. I cannot rationalize her there, me here, and the astral rock grows, and I miss her walking the beach, miss her waiting for me, miss her not underestimating me, and perception tilts, it will never, now, stop tilting.

IDEAS OF HAPPINESS

The start of the storm is the sound of a chair being trawled across a garage floor. The color of everything except the sky is flicker. Some of the birch tree leaves have turned yellow from the week's intense heat, and now those yellow bits are pulling free, snapping out, floating north, pirouetting as they float, and if they were thinking creatures, their thoughts would spin.

I watch through the bedroom windows. I wait. No rain yet.

Last week, in this room, ahead of this weather, I sat beside my son and tried not to cry, but I cried. He was home turning thirty, and he had found me here appraising the sky. *Hey, Mom.* Sat down. Began to talk. He is his many cultures—Salvadoran, Filipino, Italian, German, that thin idyllic strain of the Scots—and his black hair is thick, his beard comes easy, his body is sculpted by his many hours at the gym and the long walks he takes along the Hudson where he has, for many years now, lived. He writes police dramas for the distracting fun of it—character, smart talk, plot.

He part-times for a major-league soccer team, refs dodgeball on Tuesdays, refs cornhole on Wednesdays, builds his media-strategy business in between. He is becoming, has become, a networking genius, a tactical strategist, a man of ideas, a person powered by hope and more capable than anyone I know of superseding the disappointing outcome, of outsmarting the frustration, of saying, *There will be another day, another girl, another chance.* He has his father's cheekbones and a darker version of my eyes and his own nose, and his laugh gallops after itself, prefers not to stop once it gets going. He turns heads. He turns my head.

Hey.

Books ago, writing of him, I put down love the way I'd asserted love, the way I'd lived it, sleeplessly and forcibly, full-on and incompletely. Now I am rethinking. There's that cantaloupe-headed man at the helm, and the hot haze of the sun is ever-pressing, and the glaciers are calving, the whales are beaching, we are losing our collective shore, we open our mouths and scream across the crags of the divide, and what did I do to prepare my son for any of this—the fragility and scorch of this present time, the popped blister of our social skin, the wants we want that are denied now and will again be denied if we're not careful? What verses did I effectively deliver on piercing the truth, on protecting our soft selves, on propagating happiness?

Was love really enough?

Is love wisdom?

I see my younger self in an alley in Toulouse, my son beside me. I smell lavender and duck confit and haricot beans, I note the overhead slice of the coming milky moon, I hear a drunk mumbling a Parisian song, and I am saying, to my son, *Look around, look and see, count the details, name them.* But my son is young, he is daydreaming, my insistence is annoying, and soon I stop insisting, and soon we are just walking—me seeing Toulouse, him dreaming his thoughts—and wasn't there a better way than nothing or insisting? A better way to teach the world, its signs, its patterns, the truths we find in the in-betweens, the happiness of a borrowed song, a milky moon, wafted lavender?

I see my cold-sweat self in the car on the highway between my son's university and our home, between his move-in-day freshman self and his father and me. Bill and I are scanning the landscape for a convenience store, a gas station, a McDonald's, anything, anywhere that I might release the anxiety that has become a material and urgent thing, and I am thinking of how—after we'd dropped our son's brand-new mini-fridge, after we'd fumbled his things into the ill-fitting drawers, after we'd unevenly tucked the corners of his sheets and jaggedly walked his campus—he'd hugged us in the parking garage and waved goodbye, and I could read in his eyes the concern he felt for me, his anxiety for my anxiety, which is not the gift a mother gives. I'd meant to say, *This is your life. Live it.* I'd meant for him to return to his new room on an uplifted tide of possibilities, his happiness purified by my faith in his future, but I did not purify.

I see my stricken self in another car on other roads in the low light of a midautumnal dawn—my husband speeding, the address in the phone in my hands, the text messages that I'd failed to hear when they'd arrived in the middle of the night there, too. Out with a Philadelphia friend in a Philadelphia club, my son has been hurt, dragged into an elevator and slammed by two sets of fists and racist intent and taken back to his friend's home, swollen and bloody. When we find the right street and slow the car and our son appears on the stoop of his friend's house, there is only one eye that can be seen, only one part of his face or arm that I can look at without panic rising like bile within me. And what he says is, *Hey.* And what he means is, *Please don't worry, please don't ask me how this feels, please just let me deal with this.* But worry breeds in me, and this assault on my one beautiful Latino son is an accelerant; it becomes—it would never be my purpose, it is my undisciplined fault—my son's responsibility. So that he must heal from the bruises and the stitches and the stain, even as he tries, with greatest tenderness, to heal the outsize worry I've become.

No rain. Not yet. The twirling yellow leaves have been joined by big-winged butterflies. The flicker colors flicker. The sky grows dense. Last week, sitting here with my son, watching this sky but not this weather, I confessed. *I might have done more,* I said, *I might have done better,* for it was his thirtieth birthday, after all, a time of reckoning. He laid his muscular arm across my shoulder. He kissed me on the cheek. He listed the good that his life has become. Defended his frustrations as the glory of the chase. Spoke of the strength that comes from the wants you don't give up wanting. The world is what the world is, and his life is what he will make it, and he told me stories as proof, he listed hypotheses, named theorems, and that is when I began to cry—for the goodness that he is, for the love that hurts so much it reels like worry, for the happiness I once imagined I could give him.

Hey, he said.

And I waited.

Here's the thing. Your idea of happiness is not my idea of happiness, and happiness is not something you can give me. Love is something you can give, and, Mom, you have loved me.

The flicker colors fade. The leaves fall. The rain is starting. It falls down straight and hard and I rise and cross the narrow room and stand at the open window and smell the smell of the rain that has finally come, which is the smell, I realize, of the sheets my mother would hang on the line outside, the sheets on the day after a storm.

Happiness is not something you can give.

Love is.

And I stand here.

And the rain falls straight, and it falls easy.

FIXING BEAUTY

It wasn't like me to startle her, to catch her Elizabeth Taylor eyes in a wistful double take.

You, she almost seemed to say. Her first-born daughter. A stranger.

I'd pulled my tangled hair from my face. I'd worn something that fit. The boyish and impatient and actual in me was not, in that moment, on display, and this was years ago, when she was well and we'd met for lunch and my mother's eyes said oh, and it was temporary. Beauty, with me, always is.

Oh.

I'd had a harrowing decline into puberty. Crooked teeth. Product-resistant hair. No lessons in makeup, and so no makeup, and after I'd quit ice skating (where the beauty deficit is a judged deficit) and joined the track team (where it is not), my thighs thickened to tree stumps—a problem I assiduously cured by starving myself into anorectic brittleness. I'd achieved eighty-five pounds by my sophomore year at college. One large apple a day, one sleeve of graham crackers, a run across the city, a marathon walk in the afternoon, jump-rope drills, and still: I'd stare into the mirror and not see beauty. Beauty refused me.

What would it take? Why all the hungry sacrifices—the protein injuries to fingernails and hair follicles and bones, the harrowing distractions and the boy who tried to feed me green soup. *Try this.* Peas, I think it was, boiled in a pan on a hot plate that, for some reason, I remember propped up on the floor of his off-campus room beside the books he had borrowed for so long from the library where we both worked that the books had achieved an outlaw status: nearly stolen.

Green soup? he'd said. But I just couldn't.

Thin was the thing that I'd become, not beauty. Thin was how I floated down the hall of my first post-college job. Thin was my defense against my poor fashion choices and my hair. Thin was, maybe, how the man who would become my husband noticed me, or maybe he noticed how I listened, or maybe how I loved how he drew better than anyone else ever could, or how he sang, or how he walked, but to write that this way would be to suggest that the man I loved somehow needed aggressive admiration, desired it, and to suggest such a thing would be to lie on this page, because my husband never did, he never would, he never has needed any version of admiration; he, in fact, disdains all admiration versions. Still. He married me. A beautiful Salvadoran man with a not-beautiful American woman. A life-long glare of a disparity that other women, especially, have seen.

Funny, that. How women have always made certain that I've seen how they've seen the glare of the disparity. How they have sought to leverage it.

My beautiful husband had rules. No starving yourself. No mooning after starving. No even thinking about having a baby if you are still secretly starving. Slowly, it had to be slowly, I listened. We had our son. A gorgeous child with gorgeous Latin features. I would spend hours just looking at my husband and our son, their beauty giving me such pleasure, because beauty is (we can't deny it, I'll never deny it) pleasure.

I started writing this essay on a train. The girl beside me held a suitcase sideways on her lap, not a big suitcase, more like a traveling kit, but still the word *suitcase* came to mind. When she popped the latch, pressed powdered color was revealed, sticky pencils, tubes, and eyelash curlers. She talked to me as she did her work—about how she'd taught herself eye-lining tricks, about the fallacy of the season's new colors, about all the reasons she rarely strayed from neutrals, about YouTube beauty tutorials.

She gave me the names of the colors. She gave me the names of the tutors.

I told her about the words I'd been scribbling into my book—these words, the ones that I am writing. I told her I've never completed an expert eye lining, that I rarely get it right with blush, that my lips are too thin for lipstick. I told her I was going to New York to meet a very beautiful friend I'd not yet met in person. *She only knows my voice,* I said, and that was all I said, because it was early morning, after all, and the girl was young and I am not, and the train was doing just fine on its tracks, speeding us toward our destinations, and her eyeliner was on now, perfect. Her suitcase was closed. Her face ready.

I boarded my second train. I watched the landscape go by, the ghost of my face reflected in the window, the window like a mirror once we entered the Penn Station tunnel. The train doors opened.

I hurried up the many stairs, down the crowded streets, texting my friend, blind, the way I do, hoping not to be late, but I was— my hair flying and dampening with the heat, my shoes scuffing. My friend was seated when I found her in the elegant restaurant she had chosen, and she was tall and lithe and exceptionally beautiful, all the more beautiful for making her beauty unintimidating, for crushing any possibility of a beauty hierarchy. All afternoon we talked, first avoiding the clock, then growing wary of it, now rushing our questions and rushing our answers, and I told her about this piece I had started writing, this brief history of not beauty, and then I told her about the final stretch of my mother's life, the day I had gone to see her in the hospital—my hair swept up, a red dress on, sequins along the neckline, for I'd been dancing.

My mother had not yet had her last terrible stroke. She had thought, we had thought, she would get better. We had grown to be at ease with each other, and the hallway to her room was long, and the day was gray, and there were hardly nurses anywhere, hardly anybody anywhere, and now I was running, and when I entered my mother's room, she looked up from her bed, and nodded toward the gift I had brought (orchids, the color of pumpkins, for this was October, nearly Halloween), and she smiled.

"Beth," she said, "you look so beautiful," and her eyes filled so that their purple-green was more purple-green, and I did not say no, I did not deny her, I did not diffuse the beauty she saw by confessing its source and inevitable dislocation—another had blown out my hair and pinned it up, another had drawn on my eyes, extended my lashes, and I already knew that I would never wear the red dress again; the plunge of its neck made me nervous.

No. I stood where I was, not moving, not breaking the illusion of my temporary self, just being what my mother needed, finally and especially then, to see—a first-born daughter in a red dress with smooth hair in a gray room of hospital machines, a pumpkin-colored orchid still in her hand, lending credence to the idea that it was only my mother's illness that was temporary.

Telling my friend this story. Telling the page this story. Until the story fixed the beauty.

| AFTER | WORD |

My husband has a five-minute rule. Five minutes (preferably less) to make your case, crack your joke, romanticize your past, summarize your latest conversation. Stories should be winnowed, should be gleaned, should be lustered into being. Stories (it occurs to me; he's never said this) should be art—color, texture, and entr'acte all appreciable at once, prologue sweeping toward afterword with a clarifying rush.

But I write length, or mostly do. Or I write parts whose purpose is to find their way into an implicating whole, the choreography of the thing being the thing, the adjacencies and half sums. The rain that won't come answered, pages later, by the rain that will. The dead communicating with the living. The paw prints of the raccoon reestablished as a referent, a true one thing that—because of space, because of time—has crystallized as symbol.

When Bill and I speak of my work (and we do), I summarize, sparing him the trouble of the physical pages and their length, leaving out the news about the seams, teasing out a metaphor as proof of an itinerant theory. There is only so much time in this life, he says, insufficient hours to spare. The gist will do. The gist is enough. Identify the gist, palm on some polish.

When Bill and I speak of his work (and we do), I hold his vessels in my hands, I sense their weight, I touch the funny spouts, the oxide spills baked into the white underglaze. I turn the pages in his charcoal sketch notebooks, trace the buckles of his evaporating colors, photograph the rough stuff of his easel. His art is complex and complexly sourced. His art reverbs. His art might be summoned all at once. It obeys the five-minute rule, and besides, I love Bill's art. I fall in love with his hands and the unlanguaged thoughts in his head recurrently, a constant and miraculous surprise.

In life I have become an excellent practitioner of conversational constraint—asking the questions when I can, listening proactively as we do, easing into spontaneity with only the closest of friends. "You have two minutes to tell me your news," a friend greeted me on the phone yesterday—half joking, half needing the time to finish what I had interrupted with my call—and while the call went on, my two minutes were impressively honed. I zinged my headlines with clever details. I achieved verbal velocity without flattening the necessary melodic tones. And then, for the next seventy-eight minutes, I *hmm*ed.

Still and again, on the page, I smithereen the five-minute rule; I take my own damned time to stretch and look around. Because music is possible, I want music. Because I skated, I want ice and air for prose. Because plot bores me and knowing doesn't, I write to find out what I know, or *if* I know, or if I might know sometime soon. "Life is not a series of gig lamps symmetrically arranged; life is a luminous halo, a semi-transparent envelope surrounding us from the beginning of consciousness to the end," Virginia Woolf wrote, in "Modern Fiction." She thought it, she said it, and at the hand press she and her husband called Hogarth, the press through which she published anything she pleased as she pleased (after her first two books), she sat with the weight of the words in her hands, the Caslon As and Bs and Cs, and letter by letter she chased haloes.

"Did you realize," a thirteen-year-old asked me, in Symphony Space, two weeks ago, while we were discussing a novel I had written for youth, "that every sentence in this book you wrote is kind of like a poem?" I nodded. Shrugged. "So you did it on purpose?" she pressed. "On purpose," I said. I waited. She waited. The two dozen other students and their teachers in that room sat waiting. "Because sentences are for making," I finally said. "Sentences are the risks we take."

Mostly, while writing, I have been talking to myself—back-and-forthing particularities and prescience, edifiers and stimulants, short sentences and the semicolons between clauses. Decisions must be made, and so I must decide, and shouldn't I know by now how to decide? I have read, I have taught, I am still teaching, after all. I am working others' stories through—their first six drafts, their next dozen—their stories more demanding than my stories, their questions more pressing than my own, their need for the tactical intervention and the strategic pause dragging furrows through my brain as I stand beside them in their childhood streams, accompany their grandfathers to the symphony, chase the winter wilds of an urban cemetery, trampoline bounce to an Australian sky, watch Alabaman spiders weave. *What if?* my students ask me. *What more?* And I am the middle child too long, too unnecessarily uncertain of a mother's love. I am the writer who has built a house of memoir. I am rushing to help, and as I help, I am useful and not beautiful, interested, not interesting, necessarily absent except for all the ways I hope to help.

But alone with my prose I am maker and critic, teacher and

student, lazy and specific. Alone with my prose I fail for days and sometimes years and over the course of many drafts. Incapable of finding the truth in memoir, I turn to fiction. Paralyzed by length, I turn to poems. Bucking against short lines I turn to prose again, to truth again, to nonsequential truth because that seems more truthful. Fed up with the expectations of commercial publishing, I hurl my heart, bang figurative knees, adorn myself with royal bruises. I curl up on the couch and listen as my husband's wheel whirls and wait for a raccoon or a fox or a candy-colored unicorn to touch a paw or horn to the intervening glass, to rescue me from the moment.

Given the author's sales record . . .
Given the mutations of the market . . .
Given the political socio book buying book selling disposition of
      the present hour . . .
Given the president . . .
Given the coming asphyxiation of the planet . . .

Years ago, an editor wrote to me about a novel she was publishing; her name was Laura. The novel concerned, in part, a river that I loved; I might love that novel, too, she thought; perhaps I'd read it? I read the novel and I loved the novel and I said so on my blog, and time passed, books passed, the years went on, the existential crisis in my head. The more I taught others the less I knew about what was good and what was bad within myself. The more persuaded I became by my husband's unlanguaged art, the less persuaded I became by the sentences I risked.

By the person I had been.

By the person I might be.

The wife. The daughter. The self.

| The writer. |

I had been alone for too long inside my head. I needed—What would it take? Who could I ask? Where might I beg and not be judged?—to be just maker, not also critic, to run long instead of short, to speak as slow as I sometimes speak, one Caslon syllable and then the next?

I am speaking of my prose.

I am speaking of my life.

To explain how Laura essenced into the weight of the words you are holding in your hands would be to eviscerate the five-minute rule. It would be to turn an essay into acknowledgments, though don't all essays, finally, acknowledge? It would be to render unto me *practicality*, and that isn't my intention, that has never been my strength, it has never, despite my esteemed record of usefulness, been my final and actual interest.

What matters is this: Laura wears flowers in her hair and sparkles on her forehead, stripes on her stockings and geometry on her sleeves. She pulls apples from her trees outside and knives them into slices. She writes stories about mechanical birds and blackberry thistles, satisfies the contingencies of gnocchi, pickles onions, but I don't know how, sends a letter written on stationery she had set aside for this unknown purpose, and when I grew desperate for a voice beyond my own, when I wished to be a student, when I yearned to be read through, to be *seen* through, Laura appeared at the intervening glass door and lifted her hands. She slipped inside the divisions I had sliced between my selves.

ACKNOWLEDGMENTS

Memoir is a fixative. Put the life on the page, and there the life is. She will forever be running home across the creek. She will send (and again send) her uncle raw and banged-up poems. She will marry the exotic man and relentlessly fear her own unexotica. She will raise her only child with implacable regret and she will keep wishing she had done better, she had done more. She will despair *here,* honor *that,* leave the rest of everything absent. Her *I* becoming a *you* becoming a *we* becoming a *she* becoming her version, and from here on out she will represent that version, she will speak on its behalf, and through it.

And yet: There will always be new news about the past. There will always be living beyond the final page and the supposed conclusion. Her brother will find old photographs and present them to her as gifts—and there she will be laughing where she'd forgotten she'd been laughing; there will be her mother, more Elizabeth Taylor gorgeous than her conjuring; there will be her father, more Frank Sinatra handsome than she'd indicated; there will be her marriage, new in every single day of its pliable existence. Conversations will correct her. The forgotten will emerge. The forgotten will seem, soon enough (too soon) as the only subject worthy of a book.

A memoir is never right. Nor is the memoirist.

For the trust of those I love who gave me the freedom to try to make sense of my life by shaping it in this fashion, I am grateful.

To Ruta Sepetys, Alyson Hagy, Judy Goldman, Jacinda Barrett, Rahna Reiko Rizzuto, Debbie Levy, Kelly Simmons, Cynthia Reeves, Alexis Orgera, Jason Poole, Ellen Brackett, and Kate Moses, thank you for the conversations about living and storymaking.

To our Juncture family—those who have gathered with us on a farm, by the sea, near a river, in two gardens, around a library table, over Zoom, those who have contributed to or read our *Juncture Notes;* those with whom I have had treasured conversations, am still having treasured conversations, am still texting, am still laughing—thank you. No matter how many versions of my life get written, you'll always be there, at the core.

To my students at the University of Pennsylvania and elsewhere who have broadened my world, widened my heart, left me wet-eyed with yearning at the end of each semester or session, have grown up and are still growing up, thank you. To my Penn colleagues—especially Julia Bloch, Al Filreis, Greg Djanikian, Karen Rile, Jamie-Lee Josselyn, David Marchino, Mingo Reynolds, and Jessica Lowenthal—thank you for making room for me around your many tables.

To those who offered hospitality as I went out searching for truth, history, and companionship, and who sent me home with expanded views and a mother's palette, thank you.

To Laura Stanfill, who said yes, and whose marginalia is worthy of an entirely separate book (see | AFTER | WORD |), thank you. To Karen Grencik, whose goodness is transcendent, thank you. To Gigi Little, for her art and kindness, thank you. To Maya Myers, copy editor extraordinaire, who brightened these pages with her notes, her subtle tucks, her sensitive questions, her encouragement, thank you.

Finally and always: To my father and my mother, whose legacies are integrity and generosity, thank you. To my brother, the family archivist, who makes, of our shared history, the greatest gifts, thank you. To my son, who teaches, by example, patience, perseverance, and abiding wisdom, thank you. And to my husband, whose art I hope to one day find abiding, useful words for: I don't know how to thank you.

ABOUT THE AUTHOR

Beth Kephart is a National Book Award finalist, a Pew fellowship winner, an NEA grant winner, and the multi-genre author of more than thirty books that often appear on "best of" lists. She is an award-winning teacher at the University of Pennsylvania, co-founder of Juncture Workshops, and a widely published essayist and critic who has written extensively about memoir and traveled the country giving workshops. Essays, some of them included in this book, have appeared, or soon will appear, in *Life* magazine, *Ninth Letter*, the *New York Times*, *The Normal School*, *North American Review, Salon, Catapult, Literary Hub, Brevity, The Millions, The Rumpus*, and the *Chicago Tribune*. Her essay "Set Pearls in the Dark" is a Notable Essay of 2019 (*Best American Essays 2020*). Beth and her husband, artist William Sulit, collaborate on picture books, middle grade novels, Juncture Workshops, and a series of memoir workbooks and illustrated journals. Learn more at bethkephartbooks.com.

wife|daughter|self

readers' guide

SMALL PIECES: ON THE MAKING OF *WIFE | DAUGHTER | SELF |*

All there ever seemed to be was smudge. Broken lines. Poetic smear. Riddled repetitions. A dozen spiral notebooks each with a page or three of abandoned wreckage.

I could remember writing memoir but I couldn't remember how — how I'd summoned intimacy; how I'd sifted, white-spaced, juxtaposed: how I'd convinced myself that my own self mattered. For years I'd been consuming and deconstructing the form, analyzing and professing it, wedging my imagination through the pickets of other writers' trifles and rages, associations and fascinations, and I offer no excuse and yet I'm saying that I'd lost my own substantiated self.

Urging others to write their stories true, I'd put my words to use inside inventions.

It was in an attempt to save a novel from near-certain publishing oblivion that I overcame myself to write myself — small personal pieces that extracted the truth from the fiction. The essence, beauty, and lore of the young Salvadoran watercolorist in my hinterland story had been borrowed, in part, from my husband; I essayed my husband. The made-up Uncle Davy of my novel was a three-quarters version of my actual Uncle Danny; I essayed Uncle Danny. I essayed want and need and privilege, but my own, and not my characters'. Six hundred true words. Eight hundred true words. One thousand true words. My I. My eye. A sudden unleashing of relentless self-interrogation written across paper scraps and inside book margins in the countless pre-dawns of a manic happy panic.

The *I* I became on the page was episodic and raw, not seamless. Parts and pieces. Fragments. The crust of a relief map, the border-lines of coastal states. A contraindicating cycler and recycler of themes and topics and questions. Why had I never learned my husband's language? Was self-effacement my inheritance? What business had I making noise when I'd made noise or keeping silent when I'd kept silence, or making peace only to start another war, or loving too soon or too late and for always? It all kept coming back to me because this is what comes back when we write memoir.

Was I writing memoir?

And if I *were* writing fragments, so that they might, somehow, assemble themselves into a memoir whole, how should the pieces *actually* aggregate themselves? Form is a measure of the truth of our truths. Form is an adjudicator. What was my form?

Two hundred words. Eight hundred words. Twelve hundred words. Five thousand. One hundred. Many pieces. I experimented with a moody hierarchy of themes and called the mix *More Than This*. A rotten book, if ever there was one. I whittled, deleted, and shuffled the remaining parts so that they might approximate an emotional road trip and called it *I'll Be Gone*, and the whole thing ran aground—flat tires, broken windows. I reconsidered, rewrote, and reorganized so that the memoir itself was written as instruc-tions on memoir and called it *Juncture Road*, but the hermit-crab-bery was pure gimmickry, a form calling attention to itself.

Start again.

Start again.

The pages now held within these covers found their present form only after I returned to the much younger version of myself who choreographed her own skating routines to the music she carried in her head. Out on the ice, the much younger me listened for adagio and allegro, for consonance and counterpoint, for overtures and inversions, for preludes and postludes, for the songs in between. She didn't, of course, have the words for such things. But she felt the pause and hurry in her bones, the cycling through of harmonic motifs, the place in the songs where the skater leaps, where she accelerates, where she slows, where she riffs, where she repeats herself or comes toward herself, but from the opposite direction.

If we were out on the ice I would skate you this book.

If you asked about my process, I'd say *music.*

If you asked for a more scientific explanation I would say that the aggregation of parts that constitute this memoir reflect my belief that truth is not continuous, that stories live in seams, that we remember in bursts and find wisdom in the juxtaposed, that writing the same story twice is to puzzle out dimensions, that we must follow the telling details through fog and mist, that sometimes we are the teacher but mostly we're the student. The memoir built of parts says *Yes.* We'll never get it perfectly right; the truth is in the trying. The truth is there, in the cracks in the ice. The truth is there, inside the music.

Some of my parts still smear. Some of my lines remain broken. Sometimes I exasperate, defend, plead, wish, want, yearn, jump and fall, spin and scratch, annoy you. But that's the journey memoir takes us all on. That's the form of us on the page.

| CITATIONS |

Among the authors and books referenced throughout *Wife |
Daughter | Self*—those quoted, taught, and sometimes shamelessly
exulted—are the following:

Elizabeth Bishop, "One Art"
Ta-Nehisi Coates, *Between the World and Me*
Terrence Des Pres, *Writing into the World*
Annie Dillard, *An American Childhood*
Anthony Doerr, *All the Light We Cannot See*
Loren Eiseley, "The Rat That Danced"
Kitty Burns Florey, *Sister Bernadette's Barking Dog: The Quirky
    History and Lost Art of Diagramming Sentences*
Casey Gerald, *There Will Be No Miracles Here: A Memoir*
Patricia Hampl, *I Could Tell You Stories: Sojourns in the Land of
    Memory*
George Hodgman, *Bettyville*
Chloe Honum, *Then Winter*
Hope Jahren, *Lab Girl*
Elise Juska, *If We Had Known*
Horace Kephart, *Camping and Woodcraft*
Natalie Kusz, *Road Song*
Olivia Laing, *The Lonely City: Adventures in the Art of Being Alone; To
    the River: A Journey Beneath the Surface*
C. S. Lewis, *A Grief Observed*
Bernard MacLaverty, *Midwinter Break*
Hisham Matar, *The Return*
Alice McDermott, *The Ninth Hour*
Rebecca Mead, *My Life in Middlemarch*
Richard Merryman, *Andrew Wyeth*
David Michaelis, *N. C. Wyeth*
Michael Ondaatje, *Running in the Family; Warlight*
Dawn Raffel, *The Secret Life of Objects*

Max Ritvo and Sarah Ruhl, *Letters from Max: A Book of Friendship*
Abigail Thomas, *What Comes Next and How to Like It*
Sallie Tisdale, *Violation*
Inara Verzemnieks, *Among the Living and the Dead: A Tale of Exile
    and Homecoming on the War Roads of Europe*
Walt Whitman, *"Song of Myself"*
Virginia Woolf, "A Sketch of the Past"; "Modern Fiction"

Throughout the book I have also alluded to some of my own
work. In the order of their publication, those books are these: *Into
the Tangle of Friendship: A Memoir of the Things That Matter; Still
Love in Strange Places; Seeing Past Z: Nurturing the Imagination in
a Fast-Forward World; Ghosts in the Garden: Reflections on Endings,
Beginnings, and the Unearthing of Self; Flow: The Life and Times of
Philadelphia's Schuylkill River; Undercover; Handling the Truth: On
the Writing of Memoir; This Is the Story of You; Tell the Truth. Make
It Matter.: A Memoir Writing Workbook; Wild Blues; Strike the Empty:
Notes for Readers, Writers, and Teachers of Memoir; The Great Upending;
Cloud Hopper;* and *I Will Paint It!: Henriette Wyeth's World.*

| CREDITS |

The writer wishes to thank the editors of the following publications, in which some of these essays or fragments of these essays first appeared—often in slightly (or more than slightly) different forms and sometimes with different titles:

Brevity: "Paynes Gray"
Catapult: "Double Parentheses," "Here If You Need Me,"
    "Collisions"
Literary Hub: "The Four Times I Became a Teacher"
Ninth Letter: "Lily Lake"
Ruminate Blog: "Baby Shoes"
The Normal School: "Panic Attack"
The Pennsylvania Gazette: "Family Resemblance"
The Philadelphia Inquirer: "Cut the Light"
The Woven Tale Press: "Clean," "Fixing Beauty"